Collins

Fieldwork for GCSE Geography

Jack and Meg Gillett

William Collins' dream of knowledge for all began with the publication of his first book in 1819. A self-educated mill worker, he not only enriched millions of lives, but also founded a flourishing publishing house. Today, staying true to this spirit, Collins books are packed with inspiration, innovation and practical expertise. They place you at the centre of a world of possibility and give you exactly what you need to explore it.

Collins. Freedom to teach.

Published by Collins
An imprint of HarperCollins *Publishers*
1 London Bridge Street
London
SE1 9GF

© HarperCollins*Publishers* Limited 2016

Browse the complete Collins catalogue at: www.collins.co.uk

Published 2016

10 9 8 7 6 5 4 3 2 1

ISBN 978-0-00-818945-7

Jack and Meg Gillett assert their moral rights to be identified as the authors of this work. The authors dedicate this book to Jill Midgley.

All rights reserved. No part of this publication may be reproduced, stored in a retrieval system, or transmitted in any form or by any means, electronic, mechanical, photocopying, recording or otherwise, without the prior written permission of the Publisher or a licence permitting restricted copying in the United Kingdom issued by the Copyright Licensing Agency Ltd, 90 Tottenham Court Road, London W1T 4LP.

British Library Cataloguing in Publication Data.
A Catalogue record for this publication is available from the British Library.

Commissioned by: **Anne Mahon**
Project managed by: **Vaila Donnachie**
Typesetting and artwork: **Jouve Ltd**
Cover design: **Gordon McGilp**
Printed and bound by **CPI, UK.**
Cover image: Chris Frost/Shutterstock, and
© Crown copyright and database rights (2015) Ordnance Survey (100018598)

Contents

Introduction for students 04

Introduction for teachers 05

1 **Basic skills toolkit** 06

2 **Basic skills exercises** 23

3 **Model fieldwork enquiry** 37

4 **GCSE skills toolkit** 44

5 **GCSE fieldwork enquiry components** 56

6 **Suggested GCSE fieldwork enquiries** 65

7 **Urban model GCSE enquiry: Rochdale** 71

8 **Physical geography GCSE model study:
   Coastal defences and processes** 83

9 **GCSE exam-style questions** 94

Glossary 101

Index 103

Acknowledgements 104

Introduction for students: How to use this book

Geography GCSE students following AQA, Edexcel and OCR specifications are examined on their fieldwork enquiry activities. This book is designed to help you answer these questions successfully by producing an excellent fieldwork enquiry project. It will meet all your needs – whichever GCSE specification is taught at your own school.

All good fieldwork enquiries follow the same structure. This is described in Section 5, which gives you lots of advice on how to complete each part of this structure to the best of your ability.

Another really useful feature of this book is the two skills 'toolkits' in Sections 1 and 4. The skills covered by Section 1 are the most basic – and most important – skills of all. These include how to get information from Ordnance Survey (OS) maps and use pictures, sketches and other maps to make your project really effective. Section 2 provides you with some simple exercises to practice using these skills.

The answers to these questions are available at www.collins.co.uk/FWGCSEGeo, but they are there for you to check how well you are doing – not crib the answers before trying to do them! If you start getting some wrong answers, ask your Geography teacher for extra help to put things right.

The skills described in Section 4 are not very difficult, but will need you to think a little harder. The book doesn't provide any questions or answers for these – so you will have to talk to your teacher if you want to check how well you understand how to use them.

Section 3 will be really useful for you, because it gives you a completely finished enquiry write-up to guide you when you start to produce your own. Sections 7 and 8 do the same, for two complete GCSE-standard enquiries.

Now back to those examination questions! One of your three Year 11 examinations will include some questions about your own finished enquiry write-up. These questions can be based on *any* part of your enquiry, so it is vital that every part is completed as well and as fully as possible. To prepare you for this, Section 9 provides a number of typical GCSE examination questions. Where possible, the answers to those questions are available at www.collins.co.uk/FWGCSEGeo. The Glossary gives the meanings of the most important geographical terms used in this book.

Use the book's Contents and Index pages to find the information and advice you need, but don't forget that your most important resource of all is your Geography teacher. Your teacher will give you all the help you need, because teachers want good examination grades just as much as you do. Working together as a team will reduce your stress levels, boost your confidence and make sure you have an enjoyable Examination Results Day in August!

Best of luck with your own project – and with the fieldwork enquiry-based questions in your Year 11 Summer Examination.

Introduction for teachers: The fieldwork-based examination

All Geography GCSE students following AQA, Edexcel and OCR specifications are formally examined on their fieldwork enquiry activities. These Awarding Bodies' five specifications include fieldwork-based questions in one of their three examinations. There are some variations in the specifications' examination arrangements, but this book is generic in approach so as to cater for all Geography students – irrespective of whichever GCSE specification is selected by their particular school.

Geography fieldwork can, and should, be a positive and enjoyable experience. Most schools recognise this and include some form of practical outdoor work in the years prior to their examination course. Apart from the enjoyment aspect of this activity, setting aside time for enquiry research and follow-up work during Key Stage 3 is seen as crucial to making students feel secure and confident when undertaking this type of activity at GCSE level. The old adage 'practice makes perfect' most certainly applies in this instance.

While there is no formal external assessment of enquiry-based work, it is essential that sufficient time is provided to allow students to complete all the recommended stages of the enquiry write-up as fully as possible. There are several reasons for doing this:

- Formal, enquiry-based examination questions can be set on *any* of the recommended stages.
- A fieldwork enquiry provides case study material that may prove helpful in answering examination questions not directly related to fieldwork activity.
- A comprehensive enquiry write-up provides a valuable opportunity to re-visit and revise previously taught topics.
- Familiarity with key, subject-specific terminology is expected in all examinations. Using such terminology in context should also be integral to any effective fieldwork enquiry.
- Fieldwork enquiries involve practicing data presentation skills that often feature in other examination questions and are one of the foundation blocks of any Geography course.
- Last, but certainly not least, inspectors from HMI, Ofsted, Local Authorities and the JCQ Centre Inspection Service have the right to assess how well a school meets Awarding Body expectations – including those regarding the completion of fieldwork enquiries.

This book covers every aspect of conducting and completing a GCSE Geography fieldwork enquiry. It assumes that every student will benefit from its two skills toolkits; these require no prior knowledge of those data presentation and evaluation techniques which are most likely to feature in both human and physical Geography-based fieldwork enquiries. The methods selected for the Basic Skills Toolkit are considered so important that a set of practice exercises has been provided for them. An answers section available at www.collins.co.uk/FWGCSEGeo gives teachers an opportunity for internal assessment and the means to determine whether further skills practice is required of their students.

Positive feedback on this book is invited, and suggestions made by users should be directed to the Publisher in the first instance.

Basic skills toolkit

LEARNING OBJECTIVES
✓ Be able to use a variety of ways of presenting geographical data.
✓ Be able to obtain and use information from Ordnance Survey (OS) maps.

Introduction

This section introduces you to the key skills needed to produce a really good fieldwork enquiry. You don't, of course, have to use them all – simply choose those that best display the information you have collected. The exercises in the next section allow you to practice the skills you want to include in your chosen enquiry.

Tables

Tables are an important link between the data collated by students and the presented data in an enquiry write-up. They are quick to produce using a computer and are very easy to interpret. Tables are often filed as a separate appendix at the end of an enquiry, but can just as easily be placed next to the graphs that have been plotted using their data.

When laying out a new table, arrange its data in some form of order. This can be:

- alphabetically
- in size order
- in some other logical order – like the months of the year – in their correct sequence.

The tables in Figs 1.1–1.3 give examples of all three arrangements.

Name of UK city	Population in 2011
Belfast	333 871
Cardiff	346 100
Edinburgh	464 990
London	8 538 689

△ Fig. 1.1 Table showing information ordered alphabetically.

Metropolitan area / County	Population
Greater London	8 538 689
West Midlands	2 808 356
Greater Manchester	2 732 854
West Yorkshire	2 264 329
Hampshire	1 800 511
Kent	1 784 369
Essex	1 773 154
Lancashire	1 471 979
Merseyside	1 391 113
South Yorkshire	1 365 847

△ Fig. 1.2 Table showing information ordered by number size: metropolitan areas and counties with populations over 1.1 million.

Month	Jan	Feb	Mar	Apr	May	Jun	Jul	Aug	Sep	Oct	Nov	Dec
Average (mean) monthly temperature (°C)	7	7	9	11	14	16	19	19	17	13	10	7

∆ Fig. 1.3 Table showing information ordered by the months of the year: London's average monthly temperatures.

Bar graphs

Bar graphs are used to show data that fits into different categories, such as the number of vehicles using a main road (Fig. 1.4). They are not used to display data that changes over time, like monthly rainfall during the course of a whole year; histograms should be used for these instead. Remember: bar graphs and histograms are *not* the same, so be very clear about what type of information each diagram should show.

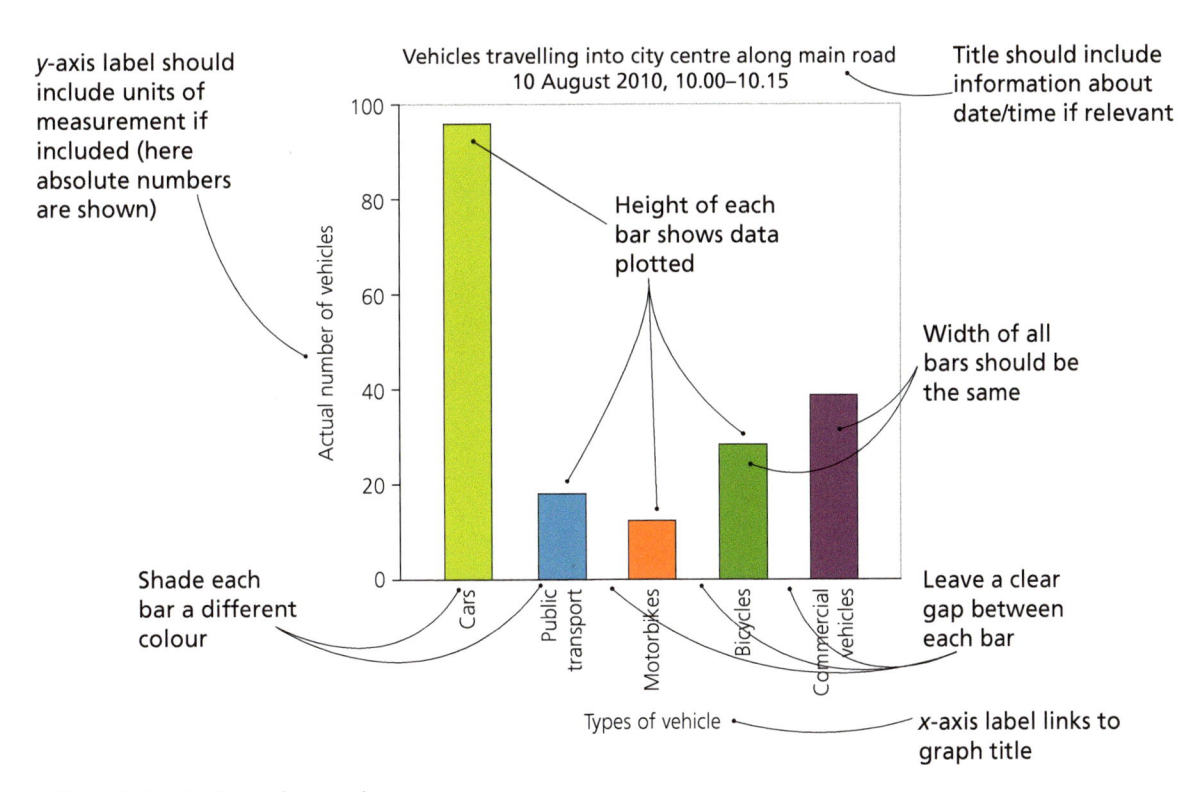

∆ Fig. 1.4 How to draw a bar graph.

Divided bar graphs

If you want to show how a data set is divided up into different groups, you can use a pie graph or a divided bar graph. This type of bar graph has a single column, with a y-axis scale divided into equal percentage intervals. The data is plotted by drawing horizontal lines across this column. The spaces between these lines are then shaded in different ways, or in different colours. A box key is added to show what the shadings stand for. The graph in Fig. 1.6 has been plotted correctly from the data in Fig 1.5. Can you see why the graph in Fig. 1.7 has not?

Number of cars	Number of households owning this number of cars
4 or more	2
3	8
2	25
1	50
0	15

△ Fig. 1.5 Data used to plot Figs 1.6 and 1.7.

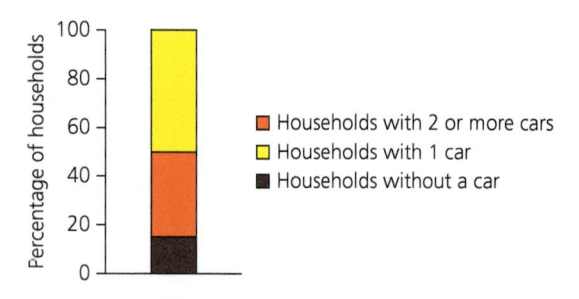

△ Fig. 1.6 The correctly-drawn divided bar graph.

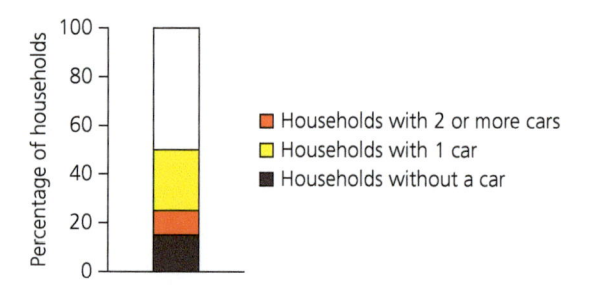

△ Fig. 1.7 An incorrectly-drawn divided bar graph.

Compound bar graphs

These are diagrams with more than one divided bar, with every bar sharing the same y-axis scale. The example in Fig. 1.8 uses percentages, but any equal-interval numbers can be used for the vertical axis scale.

Histograms

Histograms are like bar graphs, but their columns are drawn without any spaces between them, and their columns are always shaded the same way. The columns are next to each other because they show data about a continuous flow of information – like the monthly rainfall during the course of a year or an analysis of pebble beach length (Fig. 1.9).

△ Fig. 1.8 A compound bar graph showing changing crop areas in the UK, 1985–2015.

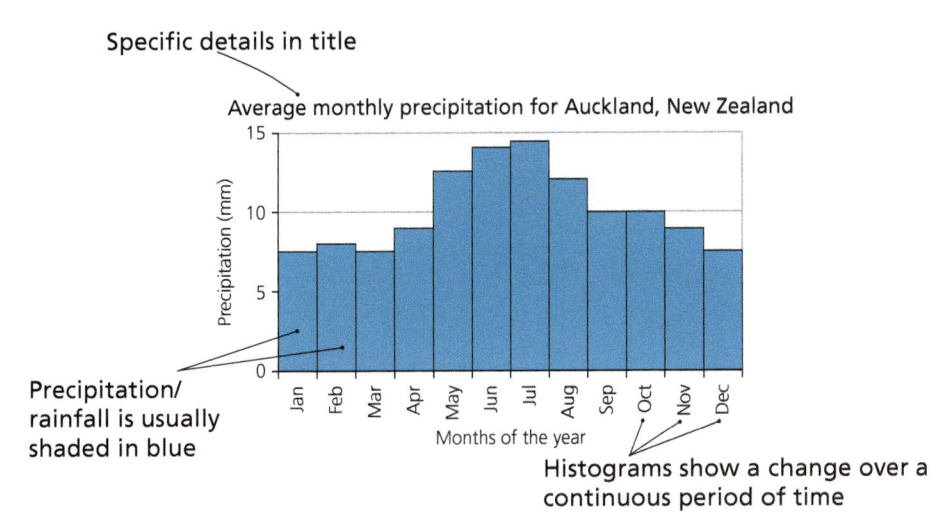

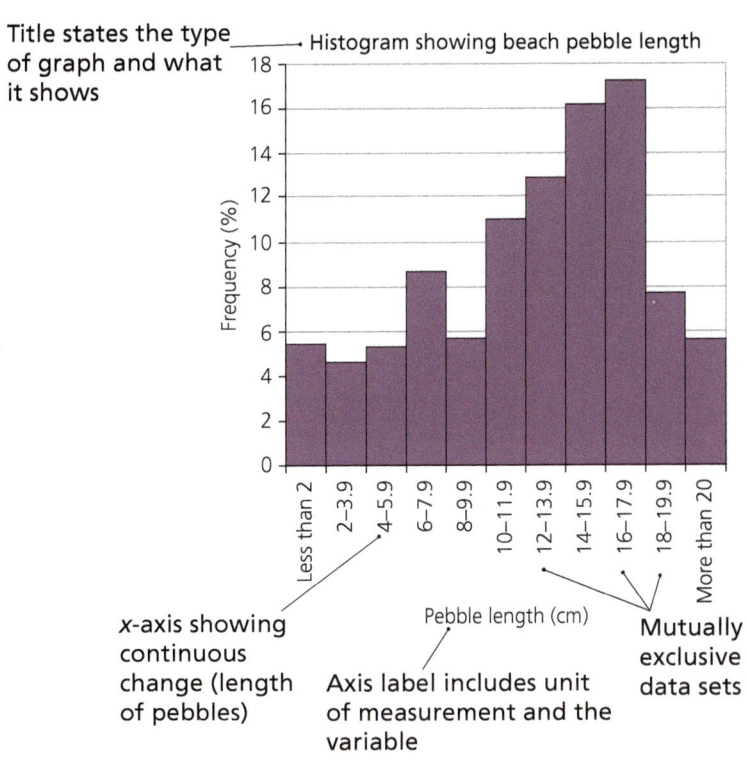

Average monthly precipitation for Auckland, New Zealand
– Specific details in title
– Precipitation/rainfall is usually shaded in blue
– Histograms show a change over a continuous period of time

Histogram showing beach pebble length
– Title states the type of graph and what it shows
– x-axis showing continuous change (length of pebbles)
– Axis label includes unit of measurement and the variable
– Mutually exclusive data sets

△ Fig. 1.9 How to draw a histogram.

Pictograms

Pictograms have a similar role to bar graphs. They have the same kinds of *x*- and *y*-axis labels, but show data by using repeated, identical symbols instead of bars. The choice of symbol shape is usually based on the type of data being plotted; for example flowers to represent the number of garden centres in a town. Photocopying symbols or downloading them from the Internet makes pictograms look much neater. Part-symbols are used to indicate smaller quantities. A key is needed to show what a whole symbol stands for (see Fig. 1.10).

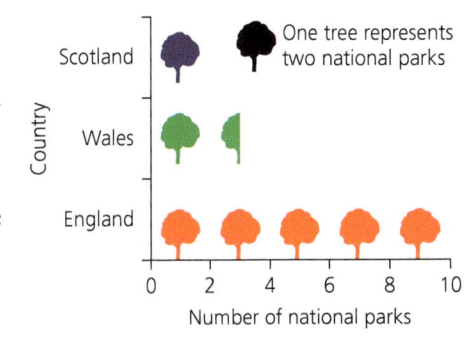

△ Fig. 1.10 A pictogram showing the number of National Parks in three of the UK's countries.

Line graphs

Line graphs are used to show data that changes over time. Time is always plotted on the horizontal, *x*-axis, and the variable data, such as temperature or rainfall, is plotted on the vertical, *y*-axis. Fig. 1.11 shows you how to draw a line graph.

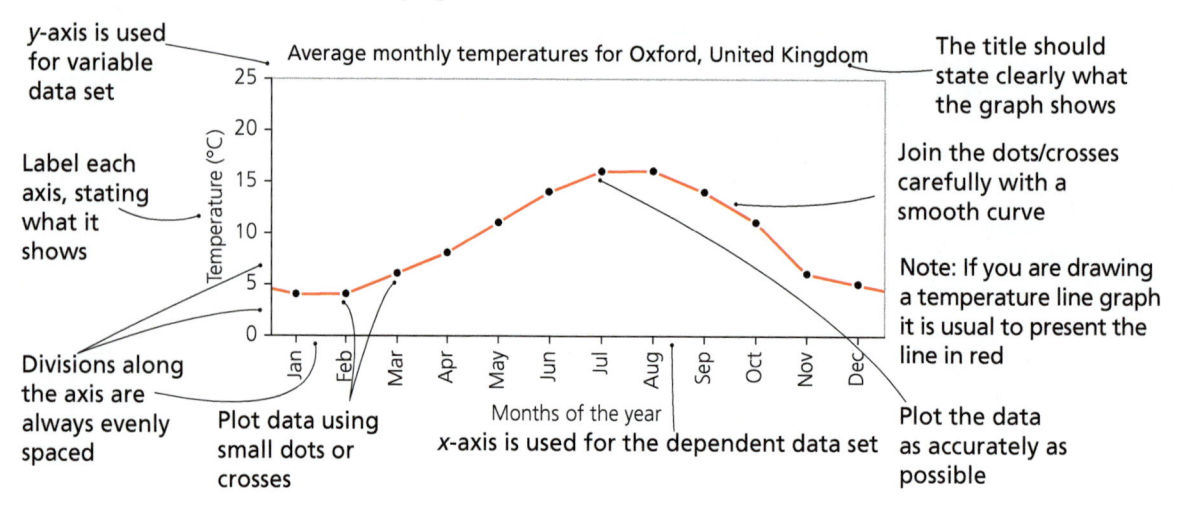

y-axis is used for variable data set

Label each axis, stating what it shows

Divisions along the axis are always evenly spaced

Plot data using small dots or crosses

Months of the year

x-axis is used for the dependent data set

The title should state clearly what the graph shows

Join the dots/crosses carefully with a smooth curve

Note: If you are drawing a temperature line graph it is usual to present the line in red

Plot the data as accurately as possible

△ Fig. 1.11 A line graph showing average monthly temperatures for Oxford.

Compound line graphs

These are graphs that use different coloured lines to compare several trends that are linked in some way. The diagram in Fig. 1.12 illustrates how the UK's ethnic population changed between the 1991 and 2011 national censuses.

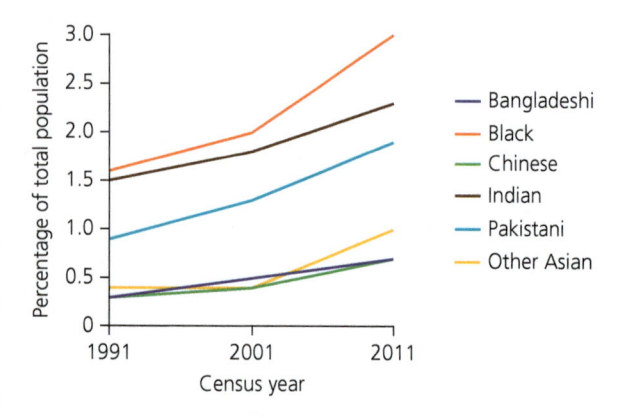

△ Fig. 1.12 A typical compound line graph showing the UK's changing ethnic population, 1991–2011.

Pie graphs

Pie graphs (often called pie charts) are divided into sectors to illustrate how a data set is divided up into different groups. This means that they can be used in the same way as divided bar graphs. Fig. 1.13 shows how to draw a pie graph, and what the finished diagram looks like, together with its box key.

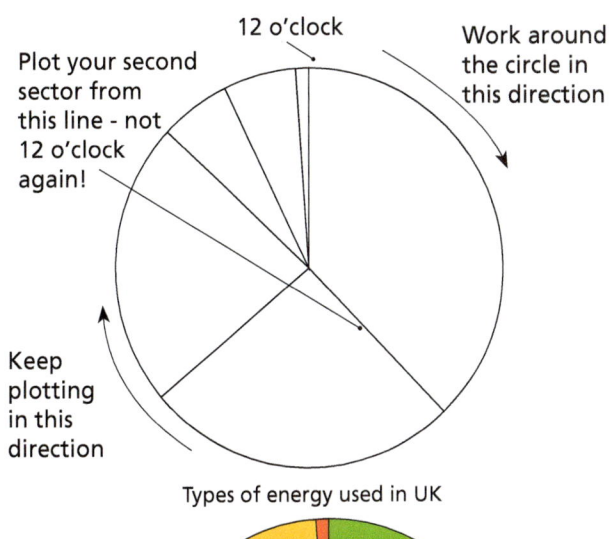

Energy used in UK	
Oil	38%
Coal	26%
Natural Gas	23%
Nuclear	6%
HEP	6%
Renewables	1%

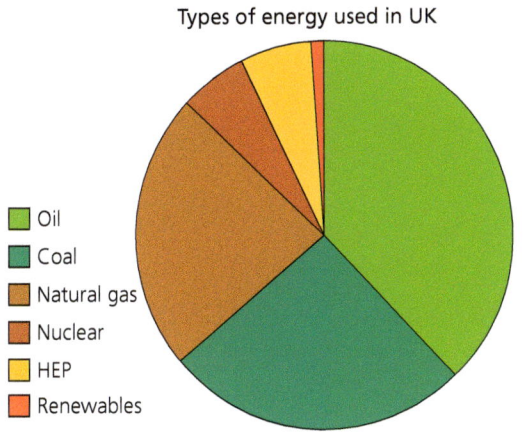

△ Fig. 1.13 How to draw a pie graph.

Map symbols

These come in lots of different shapes, sizes and colours. This table shows the main types of symbols and gives two examples of each one:

Type of symbol	First example	Second example
Drawings	Small flag for a golf course	Red triangle for a youth hostel
Letters	TH for a town hall	LC for a railway level crossing
Shaded areas	Blue for a lake	Green for a wood
Lines	Black for a railway line	Brown for a height contour
Abbreviations	Fm for a farm	Sch for a school

The area of a printed map is always drawn to scale, but only the big features, like lakes and woods, are also drawn to scale. Most features would be far too small to see on a map if they were drawn to scale, so symbols are used to locate them instead.

Maps drawn to different scales often have slightly different sets of symbols. Look at the OS symbol displays on pages 27–28 and 32–33, and you will see that this is true. In fact, some map scales have different meanings for the same symbol. For example, the letters CG stand for a coastguard building on a 1:50 000 scale OS map, but a cattle grid on a 1:25 000 scale map. You won't have to learn every symbol for each scale of map, but you will have to know how to use them.

Compass directions on maps

When using OS maps, you need to be able to give the compass directions between places on them. This is quite easy to do, as long as you remember three things:

- All the blue grid lines that cross a map from top to bottom lie on a north-south axis, with north being towards the top of the map.
- All the blue lines that cross a map from one side to the other lie on a west-east axis, with west being towards the left side.
- A compass rose like the one in Fig. 1.14 can be used to work out any of the other compass directions you are likely to need.

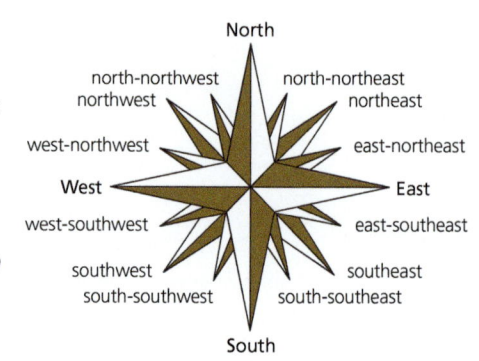

△ Fig. 1.14 A 16-point compass rose.

There are two ways of using the compass rose to find directions on a map.

The first is to imagine that the centre of the compass rose is over your starting point, and that North on the rose is pointing straight up the map. Then, all you have to do is pretend that you are looking from the centre of the rose towards the other place and 'read off' the nearest direction printed on the outside of the rose.

The second is to trace the compass rose diagram and put its centre over your starting point. This makes 'looking in the right direction' from the rose much easier.

Scale and distance on maps

Scale is the link between real-life distances and those on a map. It can be shown in three ways:

- **As a ratio**, like 1:50 000. This means that the area on the map is 50 000 times smaller than the real-life area that it shows.
- **As a statement**, like '1 cm stands for 0.5 km'. This is the scale of 1:50 000 ratio OS maps.
- **As a linear scale**, like the one in Fig. 1.15.

Note that the part of the scale to the left of '0' is sub-divided into smaller, equal distances. Using these makes it easier to measure parts of a kilometre.

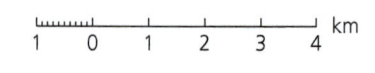

△ Fig. 1.15 A typical linear map scale.

Measuring direct distances on maps

You can measure the direct distance between two points on a map in either of these ways:

- Use a ruler to measure the straight-line distance, in cm, between them. If your scale statement is '1 cm stands for 0.5 km', all you have

to do is multiply one by the other. *Example*: 9.6 cm on the map × what each centimetre stands for (0.5 km in this example) = 4.8 km, or
- Place a straight-edged piece of paper on the map, so that both places just show.
- Then, make a small pencil mark on the paper edge by each place.
- Finally, put the piece of paper under the linear scale printed on the map and read off the distance on the scale between the two marks you have made (see Fig. 1.16).

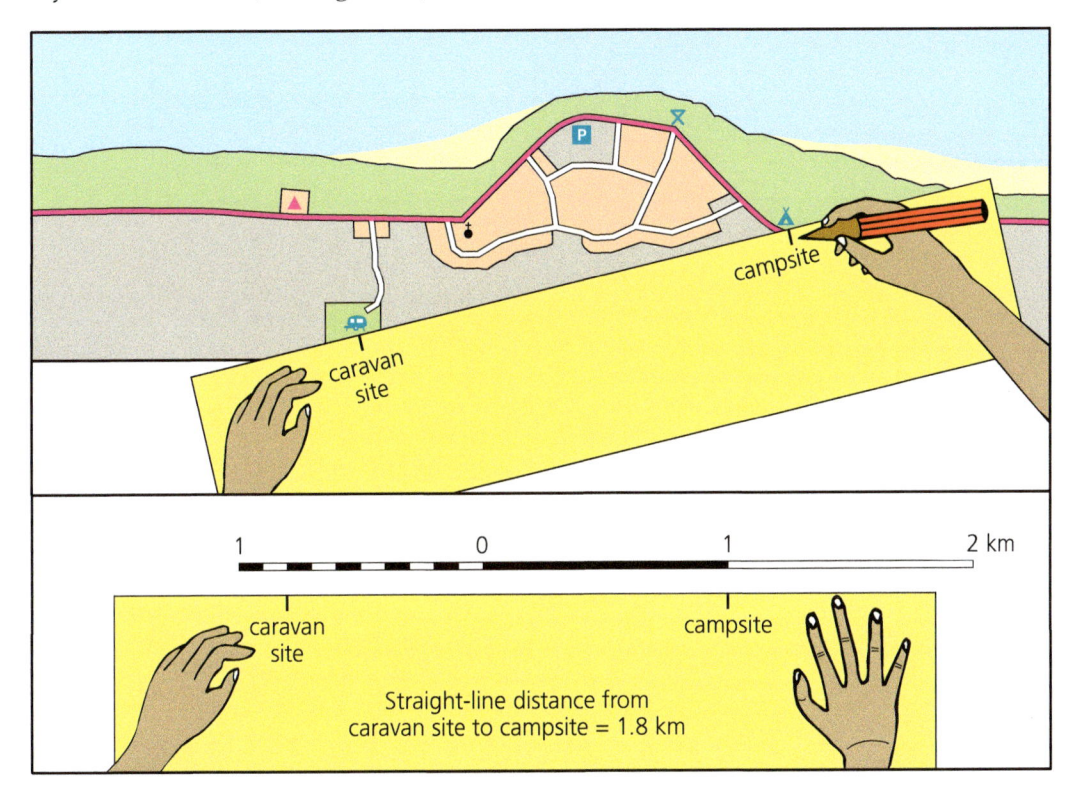

△ Fig. 1.16 How to measure direct distances on a map.

If your distance is longer than the printed scale, you will have to do some extra measuring. Move the paper backwards along the whole length of the scale until the last part of the distance on the paper is within it. You then add the final distance to the total number of kilometres by which you had to move the piece of paper along.

Measuring curved distances on maps

Measuring curved (winding) distances on maps takes a little longer, but the basic idea is just the same as the piece-of-paper method used to measure direct distances. You make a mark by the first point on the map you are measuring from, then adjust the paper at every bend along the route. Mark off the end-place on your paper, then move it to the linear map scale and measure that distance against it in the same way as for direct distances (see Fig. 1.17).

Another – and probably simpler – way of measuring curved distances on maps is to use string. Place one end of the piece of string at the starting point, twist it carefully around every bend to follow the route, then make a mark on the string where it reaches the end-place on the map. Pull the string taught and lie it along the linear scale. This will give you the distance between the two points on the map.

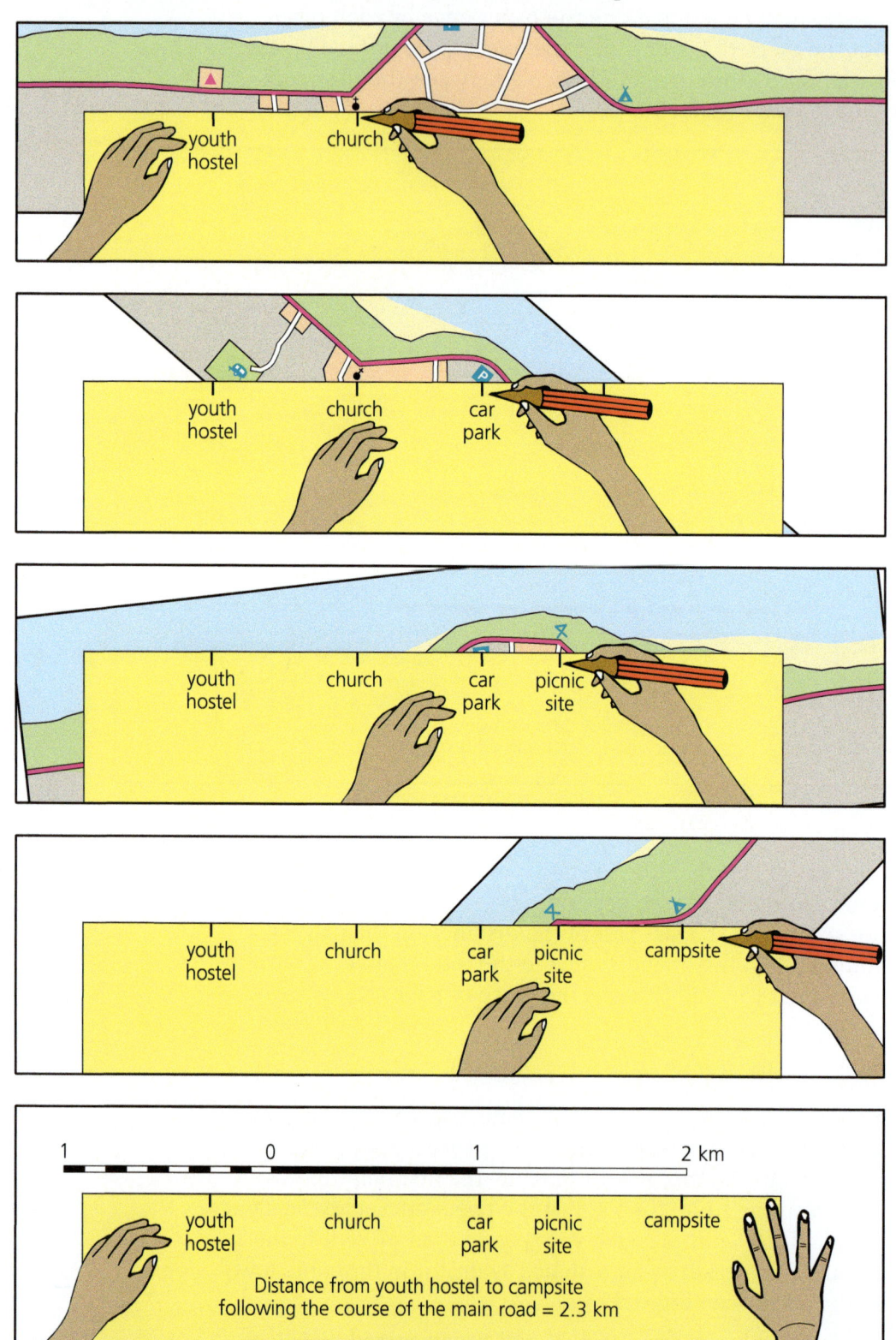

▲ Fig. 1.17 How to measure indirect distances on a map.

Grid references on OS maps

OS maps are useful to many groups of people, not just Geography students! Many people need to be able to locate places on maps so accurately that they can tell other people exactly where they are. They do this by using **grid references**.

The 1:50 000 and 1:25 000 scale series of OS maps cover the whole of Great Britain. Every map in each series has a grid of light blue vertical and horizontal lines across its area. These grid lines are exactly 1 km apart, so all the squares they form are exactly 1 km² in area. The north-south lines are called **eastings**, because their numbers increase towards the east. The west-east lines are called **northings**, as their numbers increase further up the map. These numbers are printed around the map edges, next to their lines.

These numbers are used to locate individual grid squares and places inside them. Large features like lakes and woods can be located using whole squares: by the **four-figure grid reference** system. Fig. 1.18 shows you, step-by-step, how to do this.

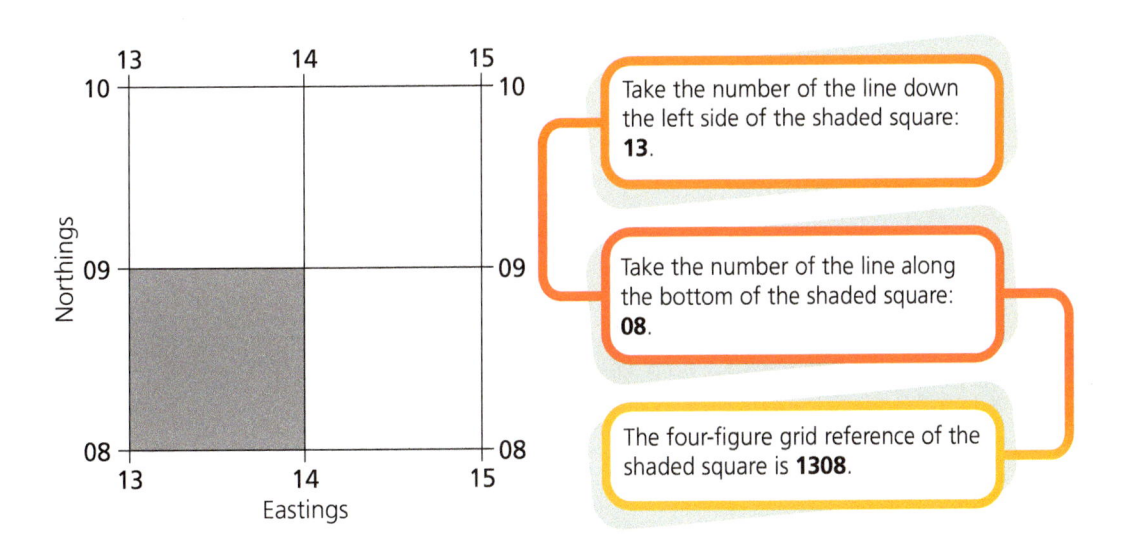

△ Fig. 1.18 How to obtain four-figure grid references from an OS map.

Smaller map features like churches and railway stations can also be located on maps, by using the more accurate **six-figure grid reference system** (Fig. 1.19).

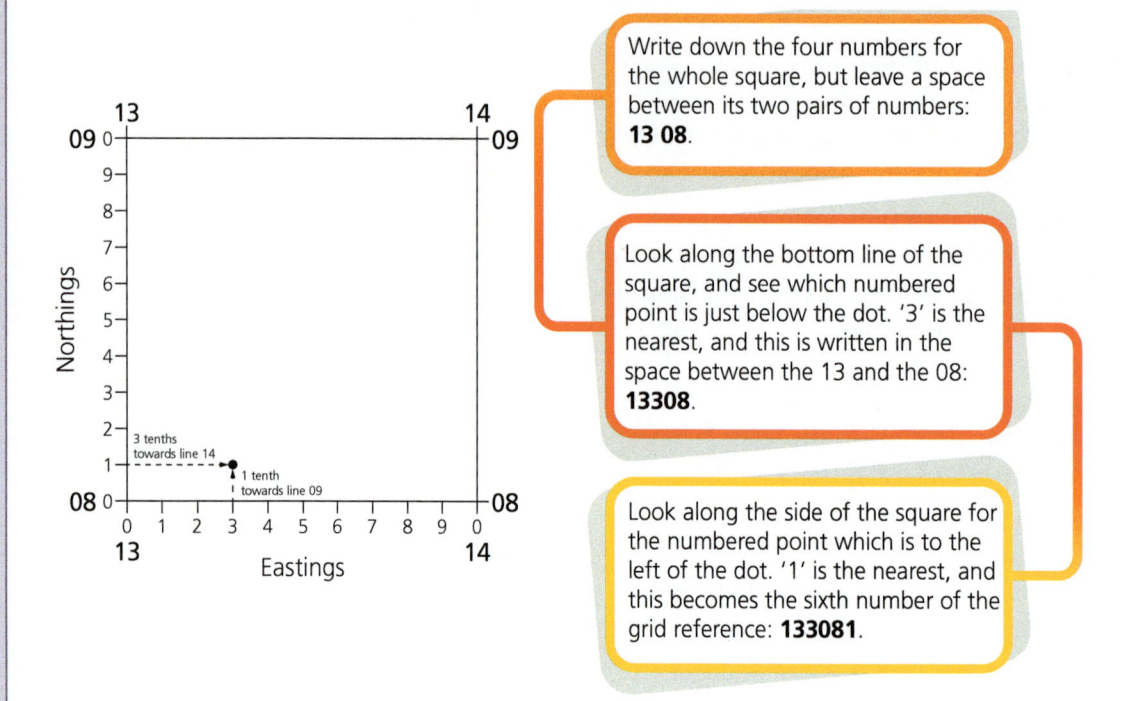

Write down the four numbers for the whole square, but leave a space between its two pairs of numbers: **13 08**.

Look along the bottom line of the square, and see which numbered point is just below the dot. '3' is the nearest, and this is written in the space between the 13 and the 08: **13308**.

Look along the side of the square for the numbered point which is to the left of the dot. '1' is the nearest, and this becomes the sixth number of the grid reference: **133081**.

△ Fig. 1.19 How to obtain six-figure grid references from an OS map.

Road atlas maps

These are an easy way of locating a survey area. They are also very useful for urban transects because the routes taken by students can be highlighted on the streets they have followed. The survey points where students stopped to gather information can be located precisely along their routes.

Many road atlases display their linear scale at the front of the book, not on individual maps. Do therefore make sure that you have added a scale – and a compass direction arrow – to each street map you use.

Examples of road atlas maps are shown on pages 38 and 39.

Isoline maps

Isolines are lines on maps that join points of equal value. Contours, used to show changes in the height of land above sea level in an area, are the best-known isolines. Two other kinds of isoline are isotherms (showing temperature change) and isohyets (rainfall). The OS map extract of the Cromarty area on page 31 shows a good example of a contour isoline pattern.

Choropleth maps

These are isoline maps, but with the areas between their lines shaded in. Any colours used for these areas should become darker as the numbers they show increase. Also, try to choose appropriate colours whenever possible, such as greens for lowlands and browns, then yellows for higher land.

Choropleth maps are often used in atlases to show how the **relief** (the height and shape) of the land changes over an area. Fig. 1.20 is part of a relief map of the United Kingdom.

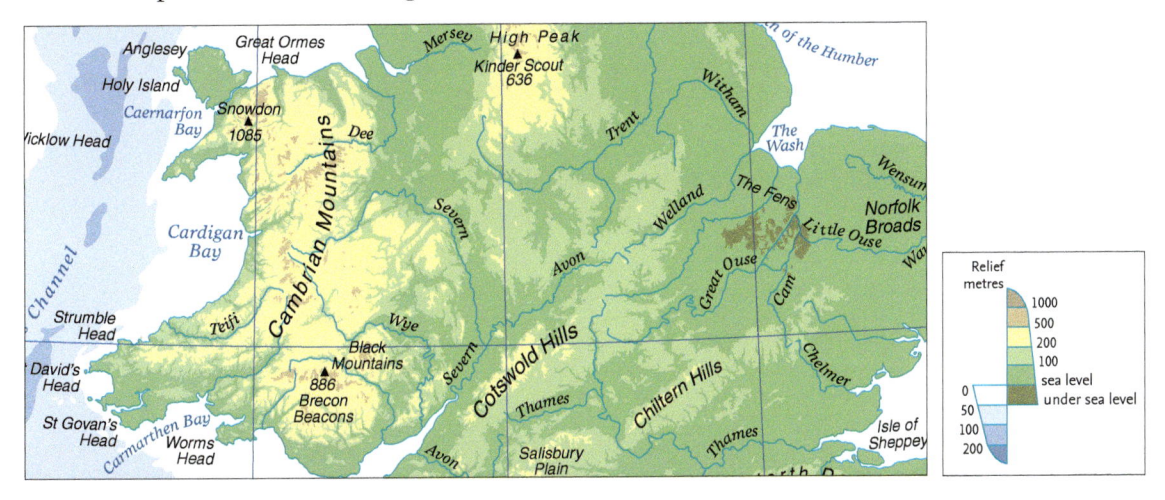

△ Fig. 1.20 A choropleth relief map of Wales.

Urban transects

Large urban areas are difficult to survey, because their streets often lie in different directions and their buildings can be all shapes and sizes and have lots of different uses. That is why transect surveys are so popular. They follow direct routes across an urban area, often along its main roads, and can show how the land use changes between places in a town. The transect in Figs 1.21 and 1.22 is quite a short one, but does provide some useful information about this part of Morecambe, a coastal holiday resort in northwest England.

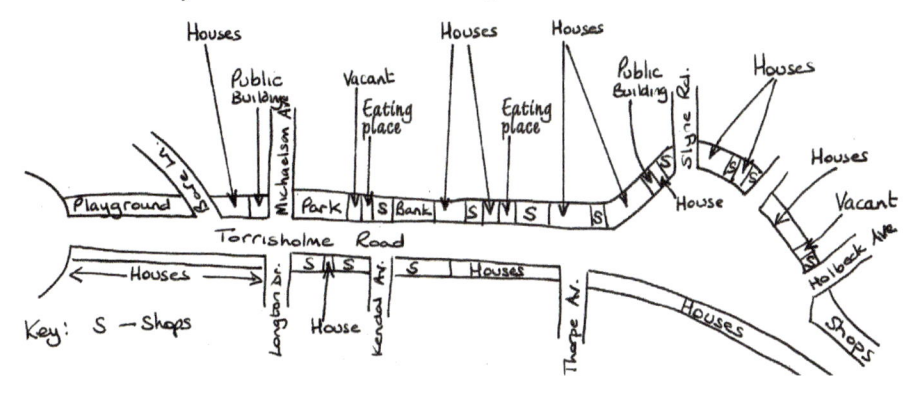

△ Fig. 1.21 Rough transect map of part of Morecambe.

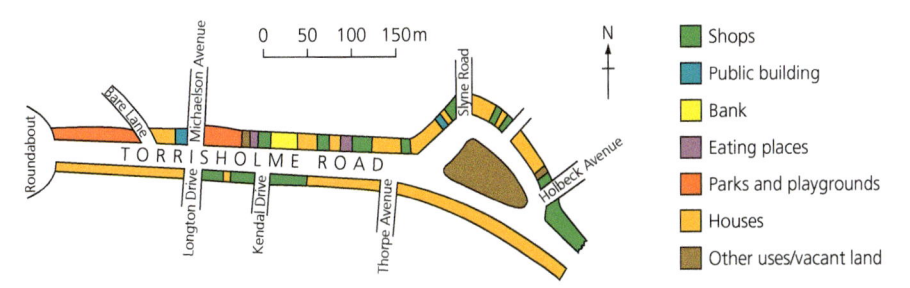

△ Fig. 1.22 Completed transect map of part of Morecambe.

Using pictures

Pictures can tell us a great deal about a place, and what is happening in it. They are available in many forms, not just the photographs you take during outside visits. Postcards and newspapers are widely available, cheap to buy, and often give excellent views of well-known features. Historical pictures can be studied in reference libraries.

If you do include photographs in your enquiry file, you must *use* them in some way. The only places where you can simply stick them in as 'pretty pictures' is on the front cover and title page of your file. Everywhere else, you must make them play an active part in your enquiry process. There are several ways you can do this:

- By adding **labels**, just one or two words to identify each place or feature on a picture (see Fig. 1.23). Labels are of very limited value, because they contain so little information.
- By adding **annotations**. These are like labels, but are longer and more detailed. This makes them much more useful, because they provide so much more information for an enquiry (see Fig. 1.24).
- By using **overlays**. Adding labels and annotations can disfigure pictures and reduce their usefulness. A good way of getting around this problem is to place a sheet of tracing paper over a picture and write labels or annotations on it instead of the picture itself.
- By arranging them around a map, with straight lines or coloured tape linking places with their labels or annotations. This can make pages so big that they won't fit easily into your file, so it's better to fold them up and put them at the back.

∆ Fig. 1.23 Photograph with brief labels added.

Grazing for sheep – too steep for cows or crops

Ridge of bare rock – looks like Carboniferous limestone

Deciduous tree – because it's losing its leaves

Dry stone wall – separating two fields

Traditional farmhouse – built of local stone

Large house – could be an old church or school

Paddock for horses? Too small for farming

△ Fig. 1.24 Photograph with full annotations added.

Drawing sketches

Sketching a view during a field trip or from a photograph may seem a difficult thing to do. However remember that you don't have to be a wonderful artist to do this, because the most important part of your finished sketch is the usefulness of your annotations and not the quality of your drawing. Figures 1.25 and 1.26 provide an example of a complete, annotated sketch and the view from which it was taken. Following the advice in Fig. 1.27 will help you to do the best you can.

△ Fig. 1.25 The view to be sketched.

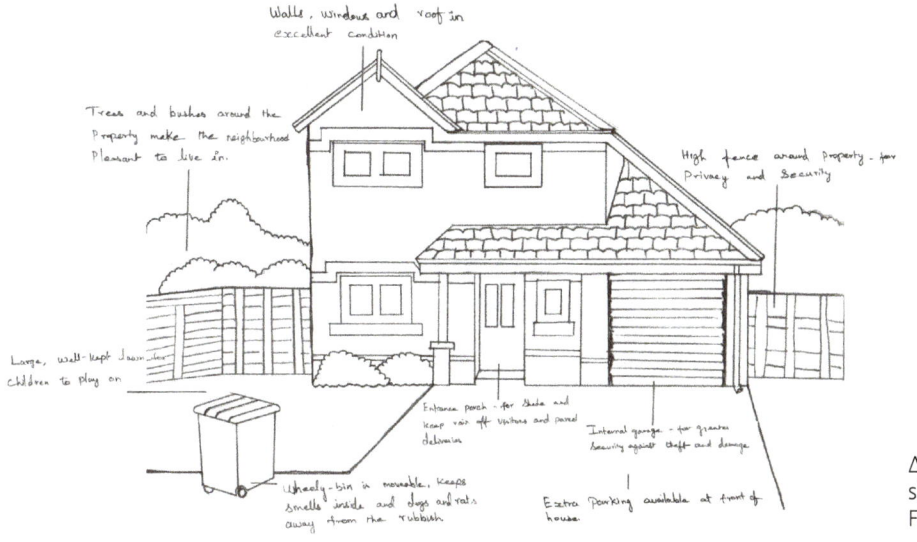

△ Fig. 1.26 Annotated sketch of the view in Fig. 1.25.

- Begin with a pencil-drawn frame which is the size of the sketch you want to produce.
- Add an upright and a horizontal line to divide the box into four equal quarters. Draw these lines very faintly, because you will be rubbing them out later. The lines are only there to guide you when you are adding to your sketch.
- Draw some major features first – like a coastline, river and the general shape of the horizon. You can add any railway lines or major roads at this stage.
- Add the outline shapes of any 'block' features such as a village, woodland, large factory, quarry and open space.
- You can then add some detail, to make your outline features look more realistic, like a church in a village or a bridge over a main road.
- Check that you have included the main components of the view which are relevant to your enquiry.
- Add your annotations, to make your completed sketch more useful and informative.
- Finally, give your sketch a title which states what the view is about and, if possible, where it was taken and the general compass direction from the viewpoint.

△ Fig. 1.27 Flow diagram showing how to draw a sketch.

Relief cross-sections and rural transects

A cross-section shows changes in relief between two places. It is like a line graph in some ways, with horizontal distance plotted along the x-axis, and the height of the land on the y-axis. You can add labels along a cross-section to identify different types of relief features along its length. These include:

- **Concave slopes**, where the land curves downwards, forming a saucer-shape in a hillside.
- **Convex slopes**, where the land curves upwards, in a dome-shape.
- **Even slopes**, where the land rises upland evenly – almost in a straight line. This is very unusual in natural landscapes, so don't be concerned if your cross-sections don't have any of these.
- **Flat land**, where there is very little change in height.

Fig. 1.29 shows how to draw a cross-section across a hill.

A rural transect may be added to a relief cross-section by locating other features along it, such as streams, woodland, villages and roads.

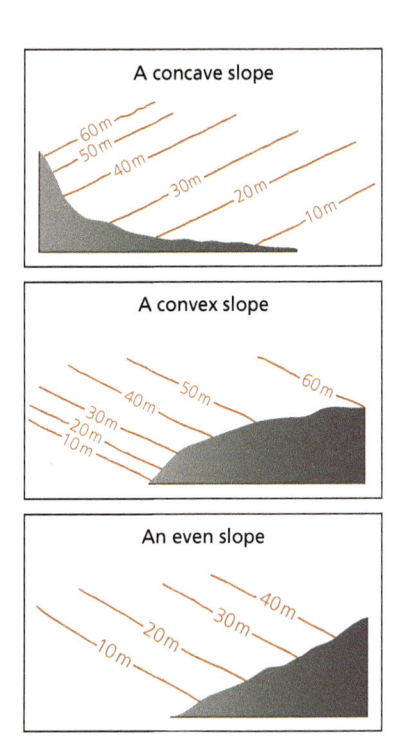

△ Fig. 1.28 Relief cross-sections and contour patterns for the three different types of slope.

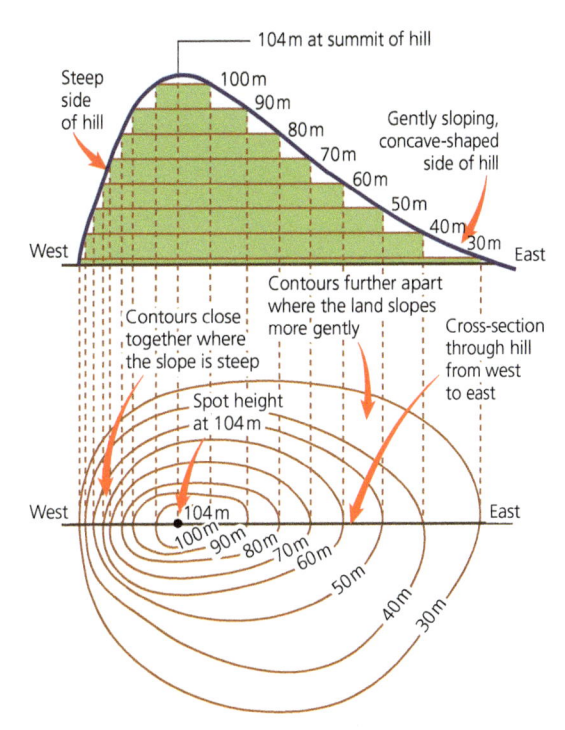

△ Fig. 1.29 How to draw a relief cross-section.

Measuring gradients on slopes

Fieldwork enquiries about beaches and river valleys often include measuring gradients (the angles of slope) of the land. This involves placing ranging poles at intervals between the highest and lowest points of your survey slope. Separate measurements need to be taken between each place where there is an obvious change in slope. Figs 1.30 and 1.31 demonstrate how to use ranging poles and a clinometer at each stage of a profile survey. Fig. 1.32 shows the correct way to operate the clinometer with one of the ranging poles.

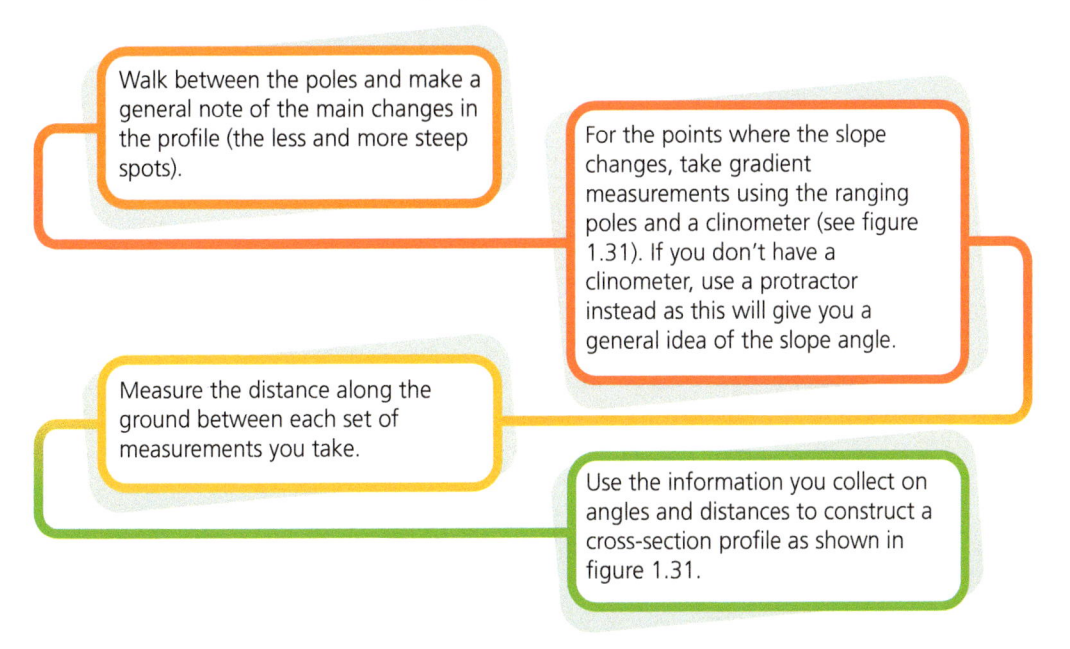

- Walk between the poles and make a general note of the main changes in the profile (the less and more steep spots).
- For the points where the slope changes, take gradient measurements using the ranging poles and a clinometer (see figure 1.31). If you don't have a clinometer, use a protractor instead as this will give you a general idea of the slope angle.
- Measure the distance along the ground between each set of measurements you take.
- Use the information you collect on angles and distances to construct a cross-section profile as shown in figure 1.31.

△ Fig. 1.30 How to measure gradients for a relief cross-section.

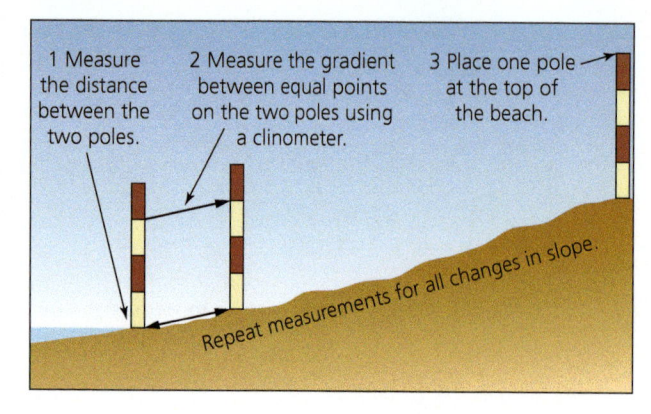

△ Fig. 1.31 How to construct a beach profile using ranging poles and a clinometer.

△ Fig. 1.32 Using the clinometer.

Mean, median and mode

The **mean** of a data set is its average. To find it, simply add up all the figures then divide this total by the number of figures in the set.

A set has these 7 numbers: 21, 16, 32, 6, 18, 51 and 45.

Its total is 189.

Dividing this total by the number of figures in the set (7) gives its mean figure: **27.0**.

The **median** of a data set is its mid-point figure. To find it, re-arrange all the figures in the set in order of size. If the set has an odd number of figures, its middle figure is the median. If it has an even number, add the two middle figures and halve this total to find their average.

This set has the same 7 numbers: 21, 16, 32, 6, 18, 51 and 45.

Re-arrange them into size order: 6, 16, 18, 21, 32, 45 and 51.

The median of this set is its middle figure: **21**.

The **mode** of a data set is the number that occurs most often.

The numbers in this set have been put in size order, to make it easier to find its mode:

2, 2, 3, 3, 3, 3, 5, 6, 6, 6, 7, 7, 7, 7, 7, 7, 8, 9, 9.

The number 7 occurs five times in this data set – more than any other number – so its mode is **7**.

Basic skills exercises

> **LEARNING OBJECTIVES**
> ✓ Be able to practice a range of skills used in geographical fieldwork enquiries.
> ✓ Become more experienced in using OS maps.

Bar graphs

1. Plot the data in this table as a bar graph. Don't forget:

   - to make all your columns the same width
   - to put equal spaces between your columns – because this is not a histogram
   - to add numbered and written labels to each axis, all written in ink
   - to add a suitable title to your completed graph, such as 'A bar graph to show…'.

Range of first letters in vehicle registration plate numbers	Number of vehicles in this registration plate letter range
A–E	15
F–J	20
K–O	36
P–T	19
U–Z	42

Histograms

2. Plot the data in this table as a histogram. **Hint:** the columns on rainfall histograms are usually shaded light blue.

Month	Average monthly rainfall in London (in mm)
January	52
February	39
March	35
April	43
May	50
June	43
July	41
August	48
September	49
October	71
November	63
December	53

Divided bar graphs and pie graphs

3. This table contains the information needed for you to plot a divided bar graph *and* a pie graph.

Type of dwelling	Number of this type of dwelling	Percentages for plotting the divided bar graph	Number of degrees for plotting the pie graph
Flats in high-rise blocks	115		
Other flats (such as over shops)	15		
Terraced houses	205		
Semi-detached houses	95		
Detached houses	45		
Caravans	15		
House boats	10		
TOTALS:	500	100	360

First, complete the table by adding the numbers of percentages and degrees needed to create these two graphs. You will have to use these percentage and degree conversion formulae to do this.

$$\text{Percentage} = \frac{\text{number of this type of dwelling}}{\text{total number of dwellings in the survey}} \times 100$$

$$\text{Number of degrees} = \frac{\text{number of this type of dwelling}}{\text{total number of dwellings in the survey}} \times 360$$

Note: make sure that you round-up any calculations of 0.5 or above to the next higher number. Any of your calculations that are lower than 0.5 need to be rounded down. Also, make sure that your totals are exactly 100 and 360 before you start plotting your graphs.

- Then plot a divided bar graph using the percentage figures in your completed table.
- Finally, plot a pie graph using the degree figures in your table.

Pictograms

4. Draw a pictogram to show the pebble-count data in this table. You could use a round-edged coin to plot the 'pictures' for it.

Distance from the sea wall (in m)	Number of pebbles in 1 m² sample area
5	25
10	20
15	18
20	15
25	10
30	5

Line graphs and compound line graphs

5. Plot this information as a compound line graph. You should use a different colour for each line on your graph and add a key to show the meanings of all your chosen colours.

Distance from start point of house survey (in km)	Number of terraced houses in view	Number of semi-detached houses in view	Number of detached houses in view
0.5	0	0	0
1.0	20	4	1
1.5	27	7	5
2.0	19	12	9
2.5	6	16	11
3.0	0	18	7
3.5	0	4	3
4.0	5	9	6

Questions 6 to 12 are based on the OS map extract in Fig. 2.1, which shows the area around the port of Goole, on the River Humber. The display of symbols used on 1:50 000 OS maps is shown in Fig. 2.2.

Symbols

6. a) List two types of *building* that are often located on the edges of towns.
   b) List two *other* types of land-use that are often located on the edges of towns.

7. a) Are there any height contours on this map?
   b) Are there any spot heights above 10 m on this map?
   c) According to the symbol display, what is the height difference, in metres, between contour lines on 1:50 000 scale OS maps?

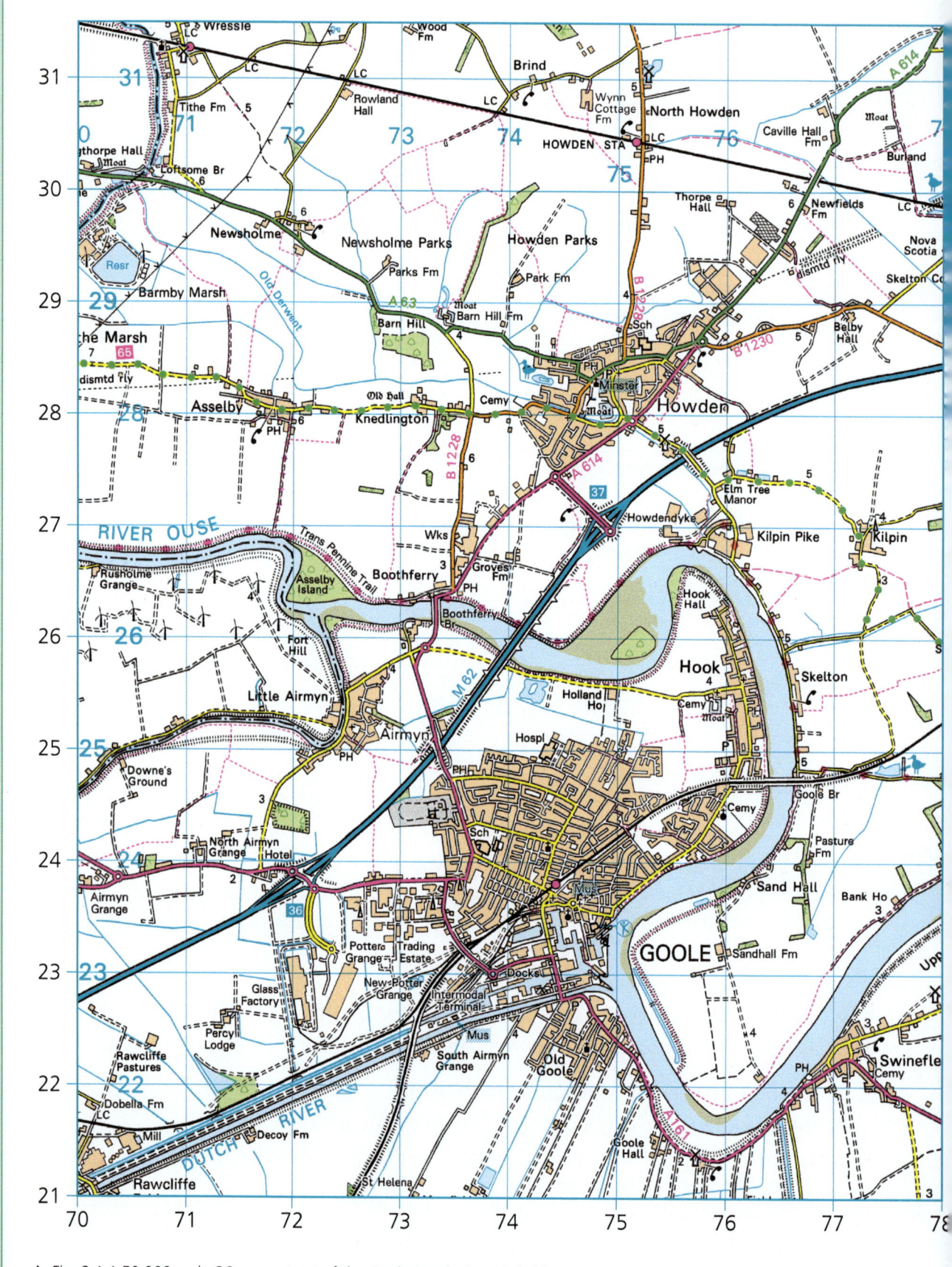

△ Fig. 2.1 1:50 000 scale OS map extract of the Goole area in East Yorkshire.

ROADS AND PATHS Not necessarily rights of way

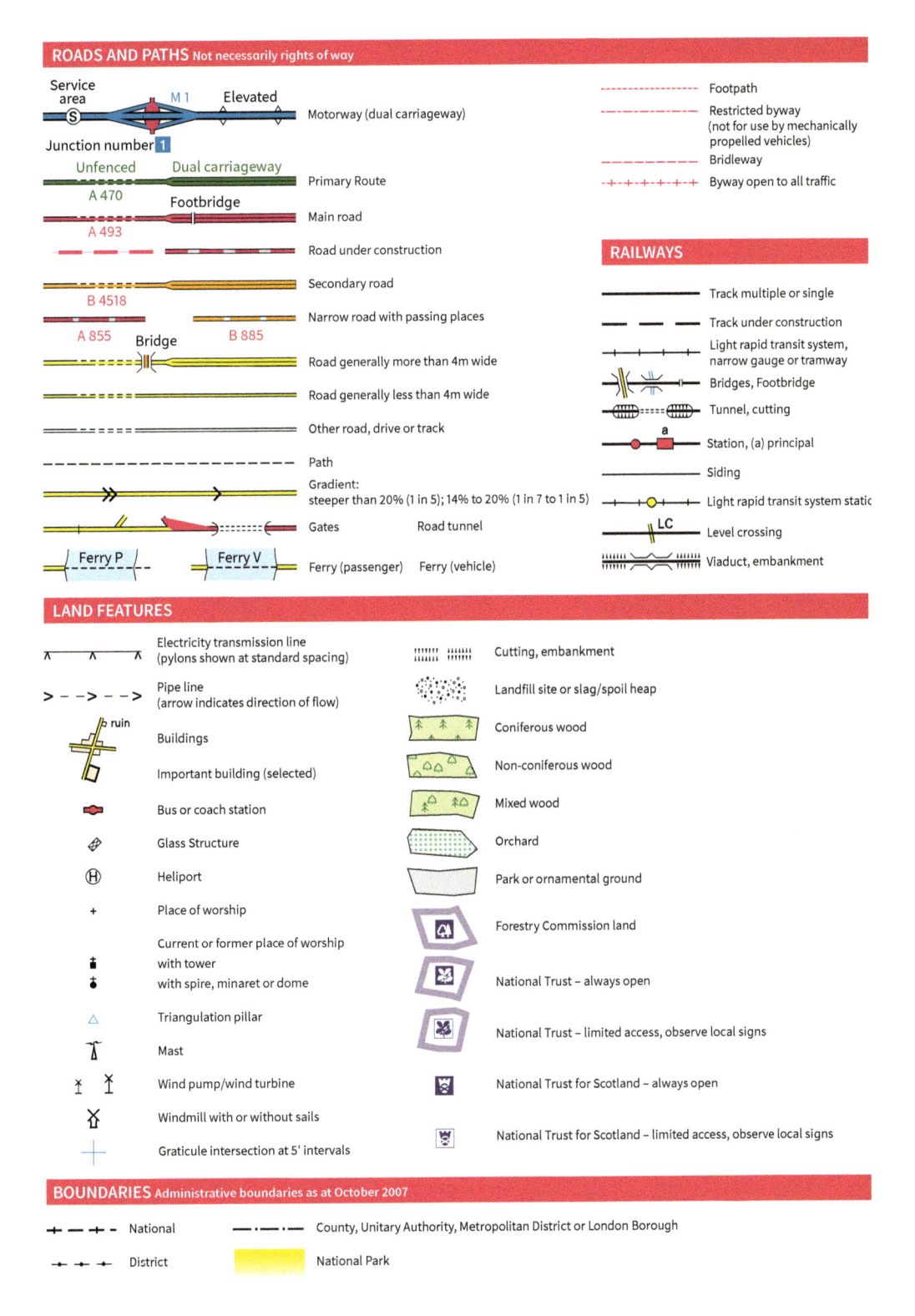

Motorway (dual carriageway) with Service area (S), Junction number 1, M1, Elevated	Footpath
Unfenced / Dual carriageway — Primary Route (A 470)	Restricted byway (not for use by mechanically propelled vehicles)
Footbridge — Main road (A 493)	Bridleway
Road under construction	Byway open to all traffic
Secondary road (B 4518)	
Narrow road with passing places (A 855)	
Bridge (B 885) — Road generally more than 4m wide	
Road generally less than 4m wide	
Other road, drive or track	
Path	
Gradient: steeper than 20% (1 in 5); 14% to 20% (1 in 7 to 1 in 5)	
Gates — Road tunnel	
Ferry P — Ferry V — Ferry (passenger), Ferry (vehicle)	

RAILWAYS

- Track multiple or single
- Track under construction
- Light rapid transit system, narrow gauge or tramway
- Bridges, Footbridge
- Tunnel, cutting
- Station, (a) principal
- Siding
- Light rapid transit system station
- LC Level crossing
- Viaduct, embankment

LAND FEATURES

- Electricity transmission line (pylons shown at standard spacing)
- Pipe line (arrow indicates direction of flow)
- Buildings (ruin)
- Important building (selected)
- Bus or coach station
- Glass Structure
- Heliport
- Place of worship
- Current or former place of worship with tower
- with spire, minaret or dome
- Triangulation pillar
- Mast
- Wind pump/wind turbine
- Windmill with or without sails
- Graticule intersection at 5' intervals

- Cutting, embankment
- Landfill site or slag/spoil heap
- Coniferous wood
- Non-coniferous wood
- Mixed wood
- Orchard
- Park or ornamental ground
- Forestry Commission land
- National Trust – always open
- National Trust – limited access, observe local signs
- National Trust for Scotland – always open
- National Trust for Scotland – limited access, observe local signs

BOUNDARIES Administrative boundaries as at October 2007

- National
- District
- County, Unitary Authority, Metropolitan District or London Borough
- National Park

△ Fig. 2.2 Symbol display for 1:50 000 scale OS maps.

WATER FEATURES

Marsh or salting · Towpath · Lock · Slopes · Cliff · High water mark · Low water mark · Aqueduct · Canal · Ford · Flat rock · Lighthouse (in use) · Weir · Normal Tidal Limit · Sand Dunes · Lighthouse (disused) · Beacon · Lake · Footbridge · Bridge · Mud · Shingle · Canal (dry)

Contour values in lakes are in metres.

ABBREVIATIONS

More information on abbreviations and symbols can be found on our website.

- **CG** Cattle Grid
- **CH** Clubhouse
- **P** Post office
- **PC** Public convenience (in rural area)
- **PH** Public house
- **MP** Milepost
- **MS** Milestone
- **TH** Town Hall, Guildhall or equivalent

TOURIST INFORMATION

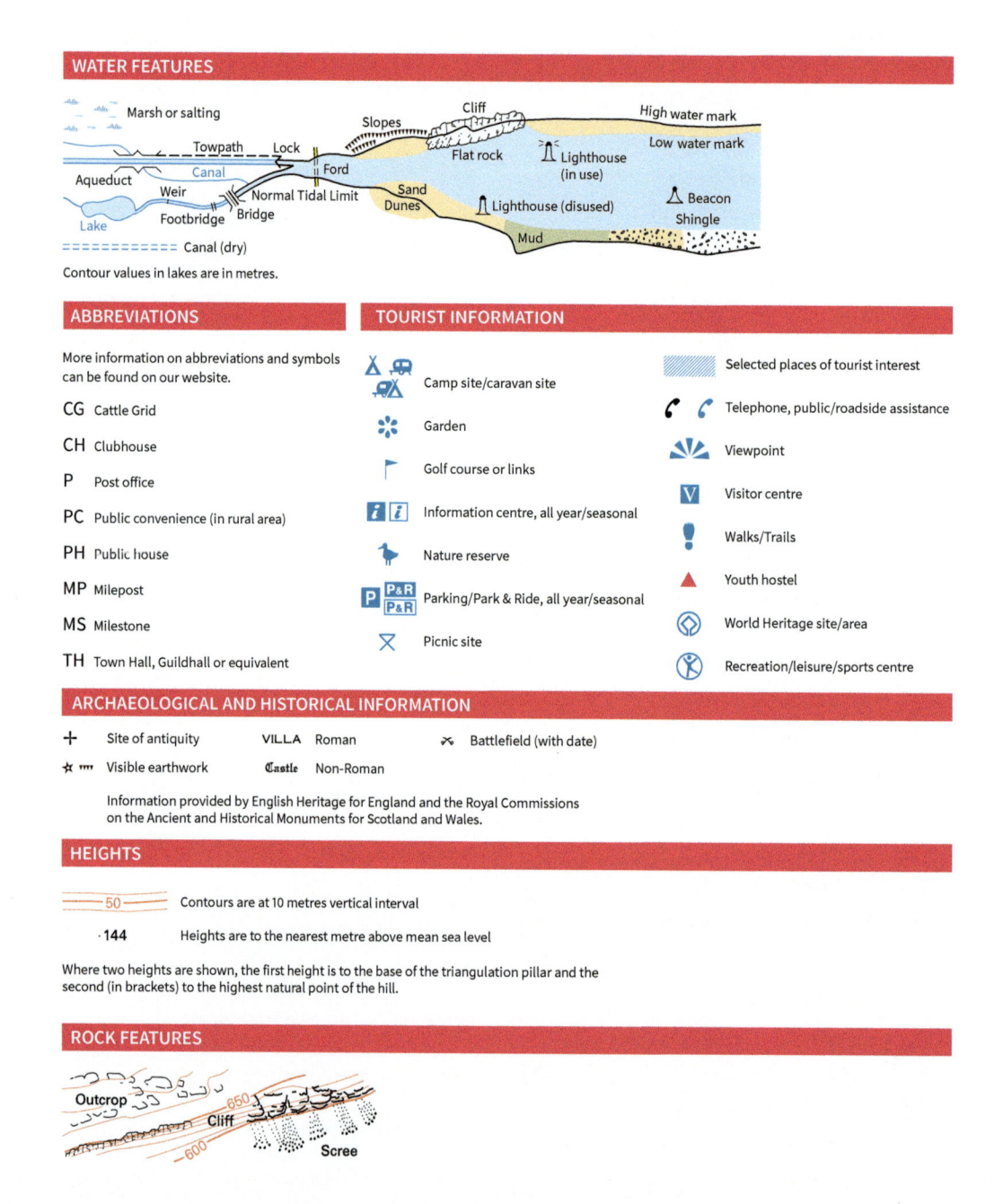

- Camp site/caravan site
- Garden
- Golf course or links
- Information centre, all year/seasonal
- Nature reserve
- Parking/Park & Ride, all year/seasonal
- Picnic site
- Selected places of tourist interest
- Telephone, public/roadside assistance
- Viewpoint
- Visitor centre
- Walks/Trails
- Youth hostel
- World Heritage site/area
- Recreation/leisure/sports centre

ARCHAEOLOGICAL AND HISTORICAL INFORMATION

- Site of antiquity
- Visible earthwork
- **VILLA** Roman
- **Castle** Non-Roman
- Battlefield (with date)

Information provided by English Heritage for England and the Royal Commissions on the Ancient and Historical Monuments for Scotland and Wales.

HEIGHTS

- 50 — Contours are at 10 metres vertical interval
- ·144 — Heights are to the nearest metre above mean sea level

Where two heights are shown, the first height is to the base of the triangulation pillar and the second (in brackets) to the highest natural point of the hill.

ROCK FEATURES

Outcrop · Cliff · Scree

△ Fig. 2.2 Symbol display for 1:50 000 scale OS maps (continued).

Compass directions

8. What are the compass directions of the following:

   a) Goole to Howden?
   b) Howden to Asselby?
   c) Howden to Kilpin?
   d) Goole to Airmyn?
   e) Airmyn to Asselby?

9. The photograph in Fig. 2.3 is a view looking over the area in the map extract in Fig. 2.1. In which compass direction was the camera facing when this picture was taken?

△ Fig. 2.3 Photograph for use with question 9.

Distances

10. a) What is the direct (straight-line) distance between Howden railway station (7530) and the railway station in square 7131?

   b) What is the total, curved, length of the M62 motorway between the west and east edges of this map?

Four-figure grid references

11. Give the 4-figure grid references of the squares in which most of the buildings in these villages have been built:

   a) Asselby
   b) Airmyn
   c) Boothferry
   d) Kilpin
   e) Knedlington.

Six-figure grid references

12. Give the 6-figure grid reference positions of these places on the map:

   a) The church with a spire in Goole's cemetery.
   b) The public house in Asselby village.
   c) Howden railway station.
   d) The only road crossing over the railway line through Howden Station which *doesn't* have a level crossing.
   e) Goole's Tourist Information Centre. **(Hint: be careful with this one)**

Questions 13 to 20 are based on the OS map extract in Fig. 2.4, which shows the area around the small town of Cromarty on the Black Isle in northeast Scotland. The display of symbols used on 1:25 000 OS maps is shown in Fig. 2.5.

Symbols

13. a) What is the height of the highest spot on the map?
   b) What is the height of the highest contour on the map?
   c) According to the symbol display, what is the height difference, in metres, between contour lines on 1:25 000 scale OS maps?

14. a) What types of trees grow in Navity Wood?
   b) List any features of Cromarty which visitors to the town could use, enjoy or stay in.
   c) Suggest reasons why there are no main roads to the east of Cromarty town.
   d) Explain why Cromarty's industrial estate has been located in a suitable place.

15. Describe the differences in these natural features between the west and east coasts on the map:

   a) The height and steepness of land behind the shore.
   b) Coastal erosion features such as caves.
   c) Beach material on the shoreline.

Compass directions

16. a) Which general direction are you travelling in going along the A832 from the 37-m spot height to the western edge of the map?
   b) In which direction are you facing when looking from the viewpoint towards Charlie's Seat?

△ Fig. 2.4 1:25 000 scale OS map extract of the Cromarty area in northeast Scotland.

ROADS AND PATHS — Not necessarily rights of way

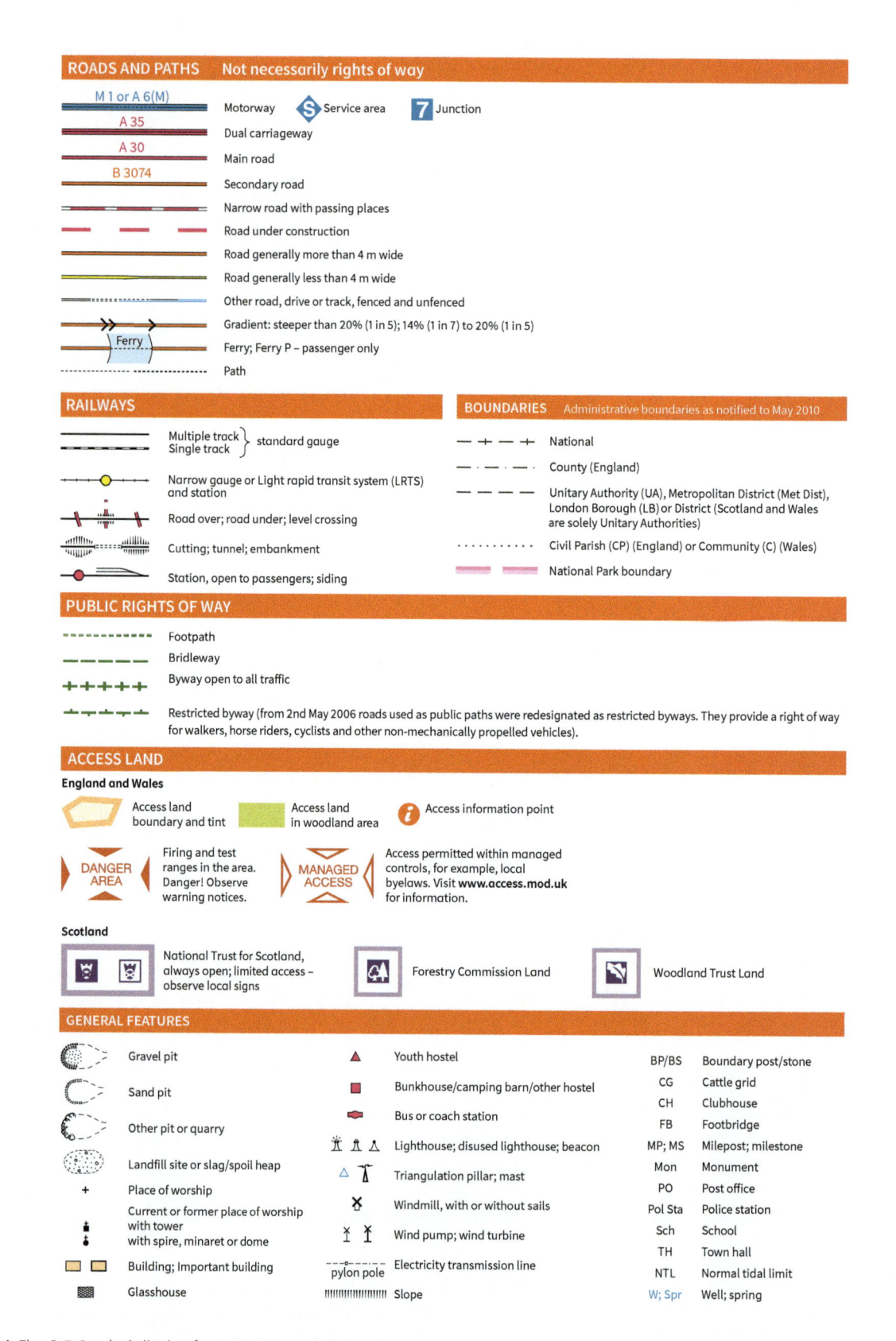

M 1 or A 6(M)	Motorway
A 35	Dual carriageway
A 30	Main road
B 3074	Secondary road
	Narrow road with passing places
	Road under construction
	Road generally more than 4 m wide
	Road generally less than 4 m wide
	Other road, drive or track, fenced and unfenced
	Gradient: steeper than 20% (1 in 5); 14% (1 in 7) to 20% (1 in 5)
Ferry	Ferry; Ferry P – passenger only
	Path

Service area; Junction

RAILWAYS

- Multiple track / Single track — standard gauge
- Narrow gauge or Light rapid transit system (LRTS) and station
- Road over; road under; level crossing
- Cutting; tunnel; embankment
- Station, open to passengers; siding

BOUNDARIES — Administrative boundaries as notified to May 2010

- National
- County (England)
- Unitary Authority (UA), Metropolitan District (Met Dist), London Borough (LB) or District (Scotland and Wales are solely Unitary Authorities)
- Civil Parish (CP) (England) or Community (C) (Wales)
- National Park boundary

PUBLIC RIGHTS OF WAY

- Footpath
- Bridleway
- Byway open to all traffic
- Restricted byway (from 2nd May 2006 roads used as public paths were redesignated as restricted byways. They provide a right of way for walkers, horse riders, cyclists and other non-mechanically propelled vehicles).

ACCESS LAND

England and Wales

- Access land boundary and tint
- Access land in woodland area
- Access information point
- DANGER AREA — Firing and test ranges in the area. Danger! Observe warning notices.
- MANAGED ACCESS — Access permitted within managed controls, for example, local byelaws. Visit www.access.mod.uk for information.

Scotland

- National Trust for Scotland, always open; limited access – observe local signs
- Forestry Commission Land
- Woodland Trust Land

GENERAL FEATURES

	Gravel pit
	Sand pit
	Other pit or quarry
	Landfill site or slag/spoil heap
+	Place of worship
	Current or former place of worship with tower / with spire, minaret or dome
	Building; Important building
	Glasshouse
▲	Youth hostel
■	Bunkhouse/camping barn/other hostel
	Bus or coach station
	Lighthouse; disused lighthouse; beacon
△ ⊤	Triangulation pillar; mast
✕	Windmill, with or without sails
	Wind pump; wind turbine
pylon pole	Electricity transmission line
	Slope

BP/BS	Boundary post/stone
CG	Cattle grid
CH	Clubhouse
FB	Footbridge
MP; MS	Milepost; milestone
Mon	Monument
PO	Post office
Pol Sta	Police station
Sch	School
TH	Town hall
NTL	Normal tidal limit
W; Spr	Well; spring

△ Fig. 2.5 Symbol display for 1:25 000 scale OS maps.

ARCHAEOLOGICAL AND HISTORICAL INFORMATION

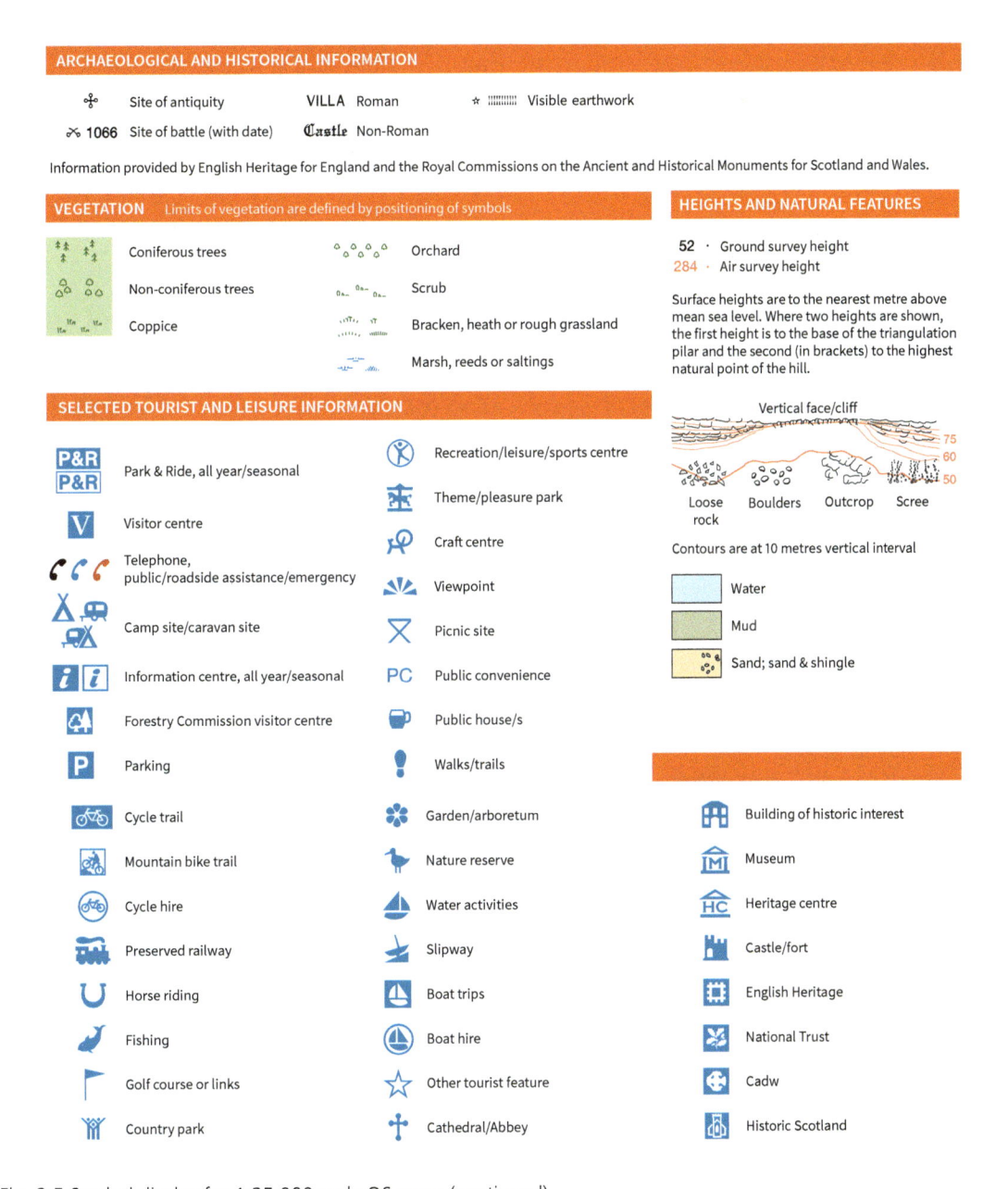

- Site of antiquity
- VILLA Roman
- Visible earthwork
- 1066 Site of battle (with date)
- Castle Non-Roman

Information provided by English Heritage for England and the Royal Commissions on the Ancient and Historical Monuments for Scotland and Wales.

VEGETATION   Limits of vegetation are defined by positioning of symbols

- Coniferous trees
- Non-coniferous trees
- Coppice
- Orchard
- Scrub
- Bracken, heath or rough grassland
- Marsh, reeds or saltings

HEIGHTS AND NATURAL FEATURES

- 52 Ground survey height
- 284 Air survey height

Surface heights are to the nearest metre above mean sea level. Where two heights are shown, the first height is to the base of the triangulation pilar and the second (in brackets) to the highest natural point of the hill.

Vertical face/cliff

Loose rock | Boulders | Outcrop | Scree

Contours are at 10 metres vertical interval

- Water
- Mud
- Sand; sand & shingle

SELECTED TOURIST AND LEISURE INFORMATION

- P&R Park & Ride, all year/seasonal
- V Visitor centre
- Telephone, public/roadside assistance/emergency
- Camp site/caravan site
- i Information centre, all year/seasonal
- Forestry Commission visitor centre
- P Parking
- Cycle trail
- Mountain bike trail
- Cycle hire
- Preserved railway
- Horse riding
- Fishing
- Golf course or links
- Country park
- Recreation/leisure/sports centre
- Theme/pleasure park
- Craft centre
- Viewpoint
- Picnic site
- PC Public convenience
- Public house/s
- Walks/trails
- Garden/arboretum
- Nature reserve
- Water activities
- Slipway
- Boat trips
- Boat hire
- Other tourist feature
- Cathedral/Abbey
- Building of historic interest
- Museum
- HC Heritage centre
- Castle/fort
- English Heritage
- National Trust
- Cadw
- Historic Scotland

△ Fig. 2.5 Symbol display for 1:25 000 scale OS maps (continued).

17. Fig. 2.6 shows a view over the area in the map in Fig. 2.4. In which compass direction was the camera pointing when this photograph was taken?

Distances

18. a) What is the direct (straight-line) distance between both ends of the A832 main road shown on the map?
    b) What is the (curved) distance *along* the whole length of the A832 shown on the map?

△ Fig. 2.6 Photograph for use with question 17.

Four-figure grid references

19. Give the 4-figure grid references of the squares with these features in them:
    a) Gallow Hill summit.
    b) Cromarty Mains farm.
    c) Most of Cromarty town's buildings.
    d) Navity Cottages.
    e) The viewpoint.

Six-figure grid references

20. What are the 6-figure grid reference locations of these features on the map?
    a) Red Nose headland.
    b) Cromarty school.
    c) The reservoir next to the A832.
    d) The summit of Gallow Hill.
    e) The exact place on the viewpoint where you would stand.

Road atlas maps

21. Find a map of your local area in a road atlas, then write down the numbers (such as M8, A832, B6318) of any motorways, main roads and secondary roads that enter, or are very close to, your area. You should list the M, A and B road numbers separately.

Isoline and choropleth maps

22. Fig. 2.7 is a type of isoline map. It shows the darker brown contour lines on that part of the OS map of Cromarty (Fig. 2.4) that is south of grid line 67.

    • Using the Cromarty map extract, write the height (in metres) of each contour line next to it on this isoline map. The heights you are looking for are 50, 75, 100, 125 and 150 metres.

- Think of what colours to use to show the differences in height between your labelled contour lines. It is best to use green(s) for the lower land and browns/yellows for higher land.
- Shade the map lightly and neatly, in pencil, then add a box-key to show the metre height range for each colour you have used.
- Add a suitable title, beginning 'A choropleth map to show…'.

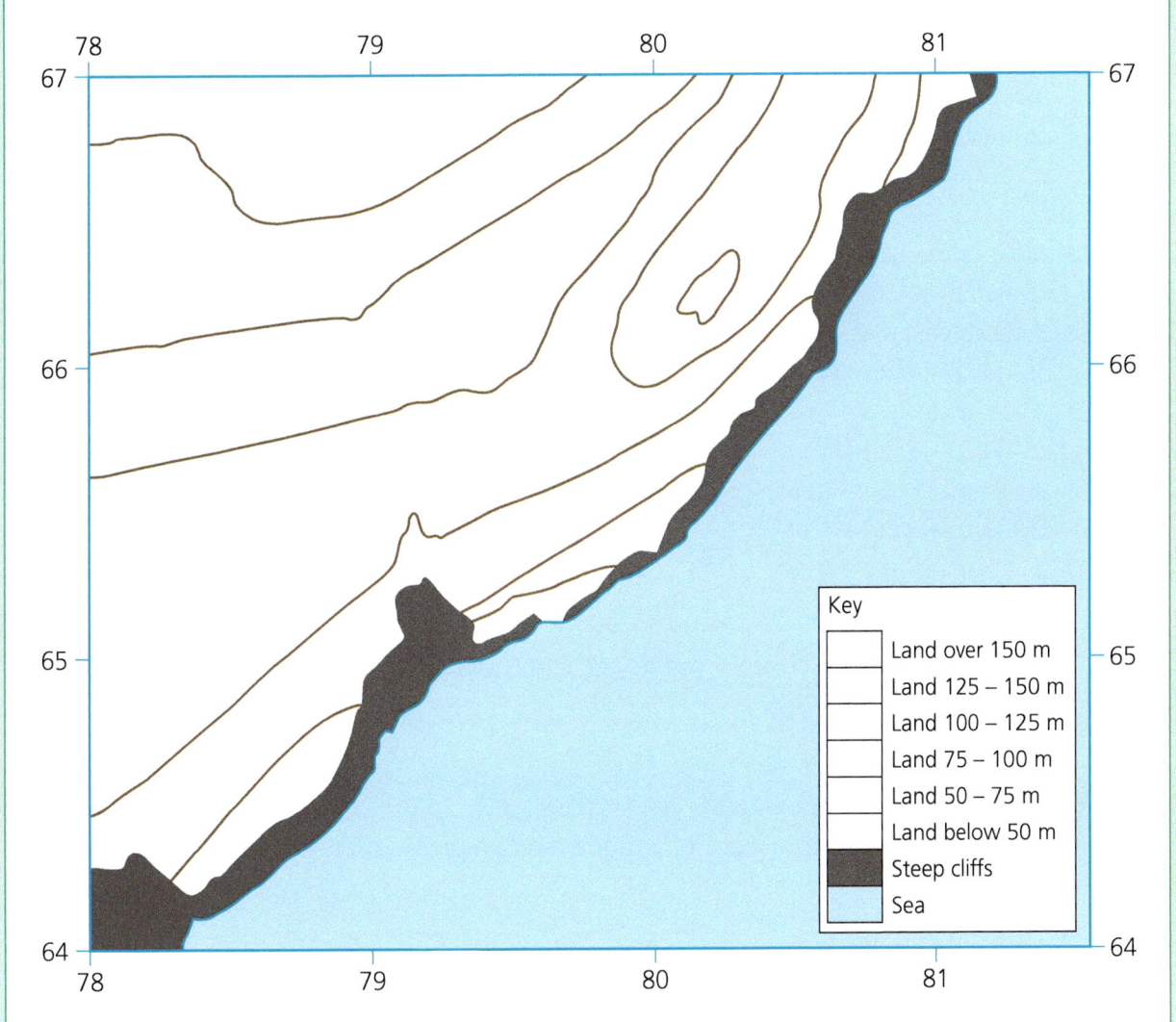

Key
- Land over 150 m
- Land 125 – 150 m
- Land 100 – 125 m
- Land 75 – 100 m
- Land 50 – 75 m
- Land below 50 m
- Steep cliffs
- Sea

∆ Fig. 2.7 Isoline contour map for use with question 22.

Picture labelling, annotating and using overlays

23. a) On one copy of Fig. 2.8, add an overlay on which at least five of its key features have been labelled.

b) On a second copy of the same photograph, add another overlay, on which detailed annotations of at least five key features have been added. These annotations don't have to be about the same features that you labelled in the first part of this question.

△ Fig. 2.8 Photograph for use with question 23.

Drawing annotated sketches

24. a) Make a line-drawn sketch of the buildings shown in Fig. 2.9.

b) Add at least five annotations to your sketch; these don't have to be written on an overlay.

Relief cross-sections

25. Draw a relief cross-section diagram between these two places on the Cromarty OS map (Fig. 2.4):

△ Fig. 2.9 Photograph for use with question 24.

- **from** the edge of the Industrial Estate at GR780669
- **to** where the 75-m contour meets the cliff top at GR790649.

The only label you need to add is where the A832 crosses the transect line.

Rural transects

26. Draw a fully-labelled transect between these two places on the Goole OS map (Fig. 2.1):

- **from** GR740300
- **to** GR780300.

All the land in this area is below 10 m, so a relief cross-section is not needed for this transect.

Mean, mode and median numbers

27. Work out the following numbers for this set of pedestrian counts, which was taken in the same place at five minute intervals: 0, 0, 0, 0, 10, 10, 100, 130, 80, 60, 50, 30, 10, 10 and 10:

a) its mean number

b) its mode number

c) its median number.

Answers available at www.collins.co.uk/FWGCSEGeo

Model fieldwork enquiry

A model fieldwork enquiry comparing housing areas in Brighouse by a Key Stage 3 student.

LEARNING OBJECTIVES

✓ Be able –to complete a geographical fieldwork enquiry to a high standard.

Aim: To compare two contrasting housing areas in Brighouse, West Yorkshire.

QUESTIONS

1. How do the two chosen housing areas compare?
2. How do their environments compare?

Geography's links to this enquiry

All villages, towns and cities are different, but we have been taught that many built-up places are like each other in some ways. I know that this is true, because I live in a terraced house and it is very like the terraced houses I have seen in other towns I have visited.

In Geography lessons, we have also been told that many urban areas change as you go further away from the centre – the zone (the part of it) we call the Central Business District (CBD). It seems likely that the way towns change outwards is often the same in different directions from the CBD. This could also be true for the kinds of housing areas that people live in.

My survey town is Brighouse, in West Yorkshire. At the last national census, its population was 32 360.

The locations of my enquiry

Brighouse is part of the West Yorkshire conurbation in the north of England. The road atlas map shows that it is in square D3, 6.5 km southeast of Halifax and 6 km north of Huddersfield.

The street map shows the locations of the two housing areas we chose to survey. The detached and semi-detached housing area is on Huddersfield Road – the A641 main road south. This is at the edge of the town, where there is some open countryside before Huddersfield starts. The other houses are in a terrace, on George Street. This is between the edge of the Central Business District and the start of the retail and industrial area just around the corner on Wakefield Road. The semi-detached house is in square D3, and the terraced house is in square E5, in the map on page 39.

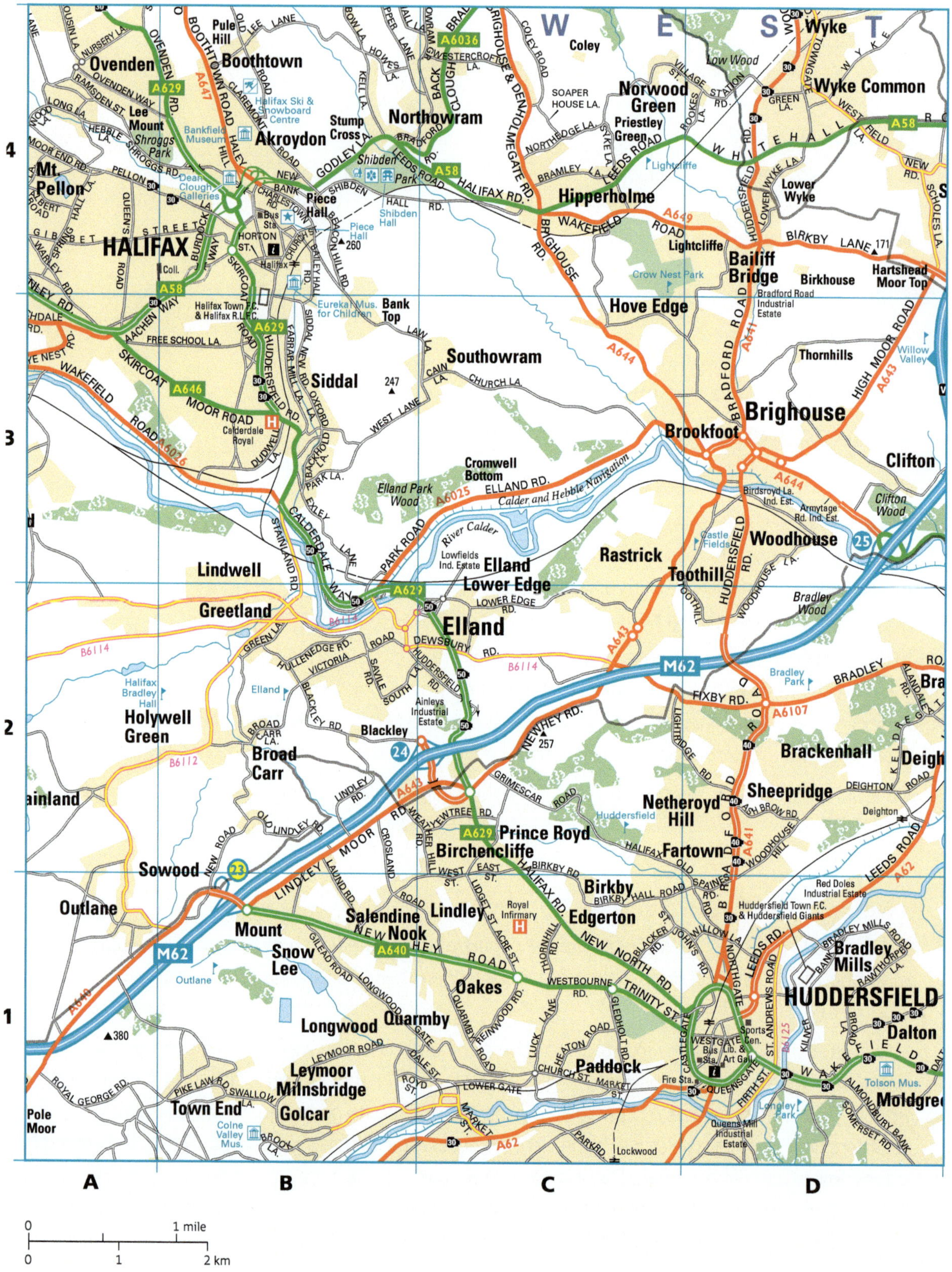
W E S T
Ovenden
Pule Hill
Boothtown
Halifax Ski & Snowboard Centre
Lee Mount
Shroggs Park
Bankfield Museum
Akroydon
Stump Cross
Northowram
Shibden Park
Shibden Hall
Mt. Pellon
Dean Clough Galleries
Piece Hall
HALIFAX
Coll.
Halifax Town F.C. & Halifax R.L.F.C.
Eureka! Mus. for Children
Bank Top
Siddal
Southowram
Calderdale Royal
Coley
Norwood Green
Priestley Green
Low Wood
Wyke
Wyke Common
Lower Wyke
Lightcliffe
Hipperholme
Bailiff Bridge
Birkhouse
Hartshead Moor Top
Bradford Road Industrial Estate
Crow Nest Park
Hove Edge
Thornhills
Willow Valley
Brighouse
Brookfoot
Clifton
Clifton Wood
Birdsroyd La. Ind. Est.
Armytage Rd. Ind. Est.
Cromwell Bottom
Elland Park Wood
Calder and Hebble Navigation
River Calder
Castle Fields
Woodhouse
Rastrick
Toothill
Lindwell
Greetland
Lowfields Ind. Estate
Elland
Lower Edge
Bradley Wood
M62
Halifax Bradley Hall
Holywell Green
Broad Carr
Blackley
Ainleys Industrial Estate
Bradley Park
Brackenhall
Sheepridge
Deighton
Netheroyd Hill
Huddersfield
Fartown
Prince Royd
Birchencliffe
Stainland
Sowood
Outlane
Mount
Salendine Nook
Lindley
Royal Infirmary
Birkby
Edgerton
Red Doles Industrial Estate
Huddersfield Town F.C. & Huddersfield Giants
Bradley Mills
Snow Lee
Oakes
HUDDERSFIELD
Dalton
Longwood
Quarmby
Sports Cen.
Bus Sta.
Lib. & Art Gall.
Fire Sta.
Leymoor
Milnsbridge
Paddock
Golcar
Town End
Colne Valley Mus.
Pole Moor
Tolson Mus.
Moldgreen
Longley Park
Queens Mill Industrial Estate
Lockwood
A58
A629
A646
A647
A6036
A649
A644
A641
A643
A6025
A6026
A640
A62
A6107
B6114
B6112
M62
A
B
C
D
1
2
3
4
0
1 mile
0
1
2 km

7
6
5
4
3
2
1
A
B
C
D
E
Red Beck
Wood Bottom Lane
Halifax Road
A641
Lightcliffe Road
St. Andrew's Church of England Infant School
Garden Road
A644
Thornhills Beck Lane
Bradford Road
Clifton Beck
Thornhills Bridge Lane
Garden Road
Brookfoot Lane
Brookfoot
Waring Green
Wellholme Park
Thornhills Lane
St. Andrew's Church of England Junior School
Halifax Road
Clifton
A6025
Elland Road
Elland Road
Bus Station
Clifton Common
A643
Calder & Hebble Navigation
BRIGHOUSE
Wakefield Rd
Huddersfield Road
Briggate
A644
River Calder
Bridge Rd
Train Station
Reins Wood
Bradford Road
Gooder Lane
A641
Birds Royd Lane
Bramston Street
Bridge End
Rastrick High School & Sixth Form
Longroyde Junior School
A643
Castlefields Infant School
Daisy Road
William Henry Smith School
Woodhouse
Woodhouse Lane
Rastrick Common
Thornhill Road
Woodhouse Primary School
Woodhouse Lane
Rastrick Independent School
Rastrick
Church Street
Ogden Lane
Jumble Dyke
St Matthew
Field Lane Primary School
Toothill
Huddersfield Road
Toothill Bank
Woodhouse Lane
Tofts Grove
Lower Edge Road
Highbury School
Carr Green Primary School
Delf Hill
Crowtrees Lane
Toothill Lane
Bradley Wood
The Jubilee Centre
Cemetery
A641
M62
Bradley Park Golf Course
A643
Slade Lane
B6114
Clough Lane
A6107
Huddersfield Cemetery
Bradford Road
0 1 2 3 4 5 6 mile
0 5 10 km

Data collection

Brighouse covers a large area because it is almost 4 km wide from west to east. This means it would be impossible for our class to survey every house in such a big town, so each pair of students chose two houses to sample – one from each area.

The semi-detached houses we chose from are on much higher land than George Street, so we surveyed them first, then walked downhill into town to look at the terraced houses. We surveyed both houses using the same sheet, but did take turns at surveying and writing down the results.

HOUSING AND ENVIRONMENTAL SURVEY SHEET

Name of road: .... Name of town: ....
Day / date: .... Time of day: ....

Tick one box on each assessment row in the table, then add and deduct any points as necessary.
Then write down the score for each survey category.
Then write down the Grand Total Score at the bottom of the sheet.

Survey category	Comparison	Best description	5	4	3	2	1	Poorest description
The dwelling	General appearance	Very attractive						Very unattractive
	Condition of doors and windows	Excellent						Very poor
	State of painting	Excellent						Lots of paint peeling
	State of roof	All slates / tiles in place						Some slates / tiles broken or missing
	Car parking provision	Has own garage						Has no garage; *also*, no parking is allowed in front of or next to the house
	If detached *If semi-detached* *If terraced* ***but***, *if a 'back-to-back' terraced*	..... add 5 points ..... add 3 points ..... add 1 point ..... deduct 3 points, instead of adding 1						
							CATEGORY SCORE:	
Any garden / land at the front or side of the dwelling	Size of plot	Very large						Very small / none
	Size of lawn	Very large						Has no lawn
	Neatness of any flower or shrub borders	Very well maintained						Has no borders *or* they're in a very poor state
	State of any gates and fencing	Excellent						Has no gates or fences *or* they're in a very poor state
	Rubbish or litter dumped on land *belonging to the house*	No rubbish or litter at all						Some big items of rubbish (such as furniture, beds, cookers and carpets)
							CATEGORY SCORE:	
The immediate environment around the dwelling	State of road surface	Road surface is in good condition						Rough surface, with many pot-holes / puddles / damage to the surface
	Traffic volume and noise	No or little traffic/traffic noise						Heavy traffic / traffic noise close to house
	Litter on pavement outside property	No litter at all						Much litter
	Public house next door *Shop next door* *Factory close to house* *Bus stop outside house* *Post box outside house* **Park/wood/farmland next to house**	deduct 10 points deduct 7 points deduct 5 points deduct 3 points deduct 1 point add 10 points						
							CATEGORY SCORE:	

GRAND TOTAL SCORE: ....

We were warned about some health and safety issues before leaving school. The main advice was for each pair of students to stick close together in case we met any suspicious characters. We also had to keep on the pavements, well away from moving traffic, because Huddersfield Road and Wakefield Road are both busy main roads – important routes for lorries and buses as well as cars. We all had mobile phones, so could contact our teacher and the school if we needed help or advice. In a real emergency, we were to run to the nearest shop or bus stop and stay there together.

Data presentation

I have put the survey category totals from both sheets into a small table. This makes the two houses and their environments much easier to compare. I have also included one of the photographs I took of each house. Both photos have been annotated, instead of labelled, to make them more useful for my report.

Survey outline	Bradford Road	George Street
The dwelling category score	28	9
Any garden/land category score	22	6
The immediate environment category score	11	3
GRAND TOTAL SCORE	61	18

- The immediate environment category score
- Any garden / land category score
- The dwelling category score

Roof, in very good condition and large enough to add extra rooms if family outgrows the house

Attractive porch, with sheltered seating area

Large front garden, with plenty of hedges and shrubs

Three impressive chimneys show that the family can afford to heat the large rooms in the house

Burglar alarm - the house is obviously worth protecting!

Detached garage, with plenty of loft space for storage

Large windows, to let lots of light into the front lounge

Very attractive garden wall and fence - gives family some privacy in the garden

Cracked, poorly painted window sill

Bollard in front of house - blocking the pavement

Litter on pavement next to house

Attractive door, in good condition - could be new

Loose wire on wall

Weeds growing out of bottom of wall

Data analysis and evaluation

The survey sheets and my points total table show a contrast between our two houses. In fact, it is a very big contrast because there is a 43-point difference in the totals!

The semi-detached house was the clear 'winner'. It was much bigger, was in very good condition and was on a large plot of land. It looked attractive and impressive, had its own garage and lots of space for extra parking. This meant that having double yellow no-parking lines on the road outside was not a problem for the family or visitors. There wasn't a single bit of litter around the house or on the pavement outside it. The houses on either side were just as attractive as this one, so our house was definitely a good choice for that housing area.

The terraced house we surveyed needed money spending on it, and a lot of litter was scattered in front of it. There was no land at the front of the house, and there couldn't have been any behind it either because it was a 'back-to-back'. Houses like this used to be very common, but most have been knocked down because they are small and don't have any spare land for parking or putting a house extension on to provide better kitchen and bathroom facilities. One of the houses around the corner was boarded up and in a worse state, so the future isn't looking good for this area's terraces. Parking was allowed outside the house for the permit holders who lived there. George Street is on the very edge of the industrial area, and there was a large carpet warehouse facing it.

Enquiry conclusions

Two questions were asked at the start of my enquiry. They were:

1. How do the two chosen houses compare?
2. How do their environments compare?

Both questions can now be answered.

Question 1 The two houses are very different, in almost every way: their size, their condition and the amount of land on each building's plot.

Question 2 Their environments were also different, because only one house had a litter problem or industrial businesses opposite it. However, they both suffered from traffic noise. The semi-detached house was on a main road and the terraced house was very near to another.

All this means that the aim of the enquiry has been achieved.

Enquiry evaluation

I think my enquiry was successful. I could answer both of its questions and fulfil its main aim as well. Also, we didn't have any health and safety issues during the two house surveys or walking between them.

My survey could have been more effective if we had done three more things:

1. Survey more houses in each area.
2. Survey some houses half-way between the two survey areas. This wouldn't have taken much extra time, because it was on our way down the hill into town.
3. Survey some housing areas in different directions from the town centre. Towns can grow in different ways in different directions outwards from the Central Business District, so doing that would be interesting and tell me a lot more about the different housing areas in Brighouse.

Acknowledgements of help received

My thanks go to my teacher, and the people who lived in our two surveyed houses – even though they didn't know what we were doing outside their homes!

Also to Wikipedia – for giving me Brighouse's population.

GCSE skills toolkit

> **LEARNING OBJECTIVES**
> ✓ Be able to collect both primary and secondary data for geography fieldwork enquiries.
> ✓ Be able to use a wide range of skills appropriate to fieldwork enquiries.
> ✓ Be able to prepare questionnaires for use with interviewing people.
> ✓ Be able to identify and describe human and physical distribution patterns on maps.
> ✓ Be aware of the potential of GIS for fieldwork enquiry data collection.

Latitude and longitude locations

A good way of locating a place within a country is to give its global latitude and longitude positions. This diagram shows how these imaginary lines lie across the Earth's surface, with 0° of latitude being along the Equator and 0° of longitude passing through Greenwich, in London. They are both stated in degrees and minutes (part-degrees, shown by a '). The latitude number always comes before the longitude number. That is all you really need to know about 'LaLo' positions, because they are listed in alphabetical order for every important place in the world at the back of school atlases. For example, the position of Bristol is given as 51° 26' N 2° 36' W.

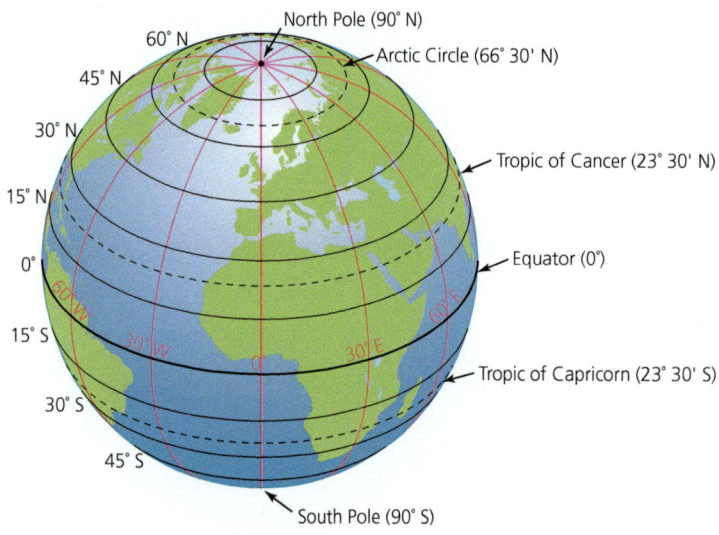

△ Fig. 4.1 This is how latitude and longitude positions on the world's surface are worked out.

Timelines

A timeline is an easy and effective way of showing the sequence of key historical events.

Events can be added to timelines in two ways:

- Those that occurred during a particular year can be labelled with a small line pointing to the time scale.
- Those that took place over longer periods of time can be bracketed together, with two lines to show their start and finish years.

Questionnaires

Questionnaires are used in interviews to obtain information for an enquiry. They can be a valuable source of primary data, but care needs to be taken when wording their questions. Suggesting and drafting questionnaires is a good exercise for students to engage in, but they should always be 'vetted' by a teacher before being used with the general public.

SHOPPING QUESTIONNAIRE

Date: ....   Time: ....

Completed by: ....

Could you help me - I am conducting a survey into shopping in this area and wondered if you could answer a few questions for me?

1. Do you live in this town?   Yes ☐   No ☐

2. Do you shop in this town
   - less than once a week? ☐
   - once a week? ☐
   - more than once a week? ☐

3. Did you travel here today
   - on foot? ☐
   - by bicycle? ☐
   - by bus? ☐
   - by car? ☐
   - other? ☐

4. How long did it take you to get here
   - less than ½ hour? ☐
   - ½ to 1 hour? ☐
   - over 1 hour? ☐

5. Did you come here today to buy food?   Yes ☐   No ☐

6. Did you come here today to buy clothes?   Yes ☐   No ☐

7. Did you come here today to buy furniture and carpets?   Yes ☐   No ☐

8. Please choose the three reasons from this list which best describe why you shop here.
   - near home ☐
   - good parking ☐
   - friendly shops ☐
   - cheap prices ☐
   - good amenities ☐
   - not crowded ☐
   - indoor shopping ☐
   - other reason ☐

That was my last question. Thank you for your help.

△ Fig. 4.2 An example of an effective questionnaire.

Here are some useful tips about creating a questionnaire:
- Keep it as brief as possible, and only ask for information that is essential to your enquiry.
- A typical questionnaire will consist of a short introduction, ideally no more than eight questions, and will have an equally short ending.
- The introduction will ask the person if they are happy to be interviewed and will state briefly what the information is needed for. Some people like to be reassured that the information they give won't be displayed on the Internet or published in a book, so reassure them that their information will simply be added to that given by lots of other people.
- The brief ending should include something similar to: 'Thank you for answering the questions, and taking the time to do this survey'.
- The most effective questions are 'closed questions'. These have a few set answers from which people can choose. Set answers like this save time back in school because they take less time to collate than open-ended questions such as 'What do you think about…?'
- Tick boxes are the ideal way to record responses to closed questions.
- Don't include any questions about politics, religion, race and personal habits, nor home addresses or other contact details.
- Don't embarrass people by asking for their age or gender. If you need information about people's ages, estimate these yourself!
- The interviewer should always complete the questionnaire – not the person being interviewed.

Population pyramids

Population pyramids are often called age-sex pyramids because of their general shape as well as the information they show. The example given in Fig. 4.3 uses 5-year age ranges (called **quinquennials**) for the central, vertical scale, but it is fine to draw simpler pyramids by using 10- or even 20-year age ranges.

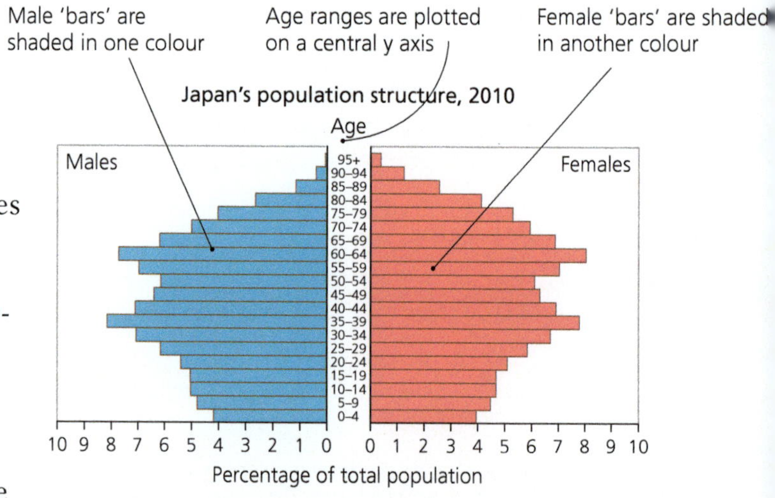

Scatter graphs

Scatter graphs are plotted in the same way as line graphs, but show two sets of changing data, instead of just one. Also, their dots are not joined up by a line drawn across the graph. This type of graph is used when one of the data sets may have been linked in some way to changes to the other set.

△ Fig. 4.3 A typical population (age-sex) pyramid.

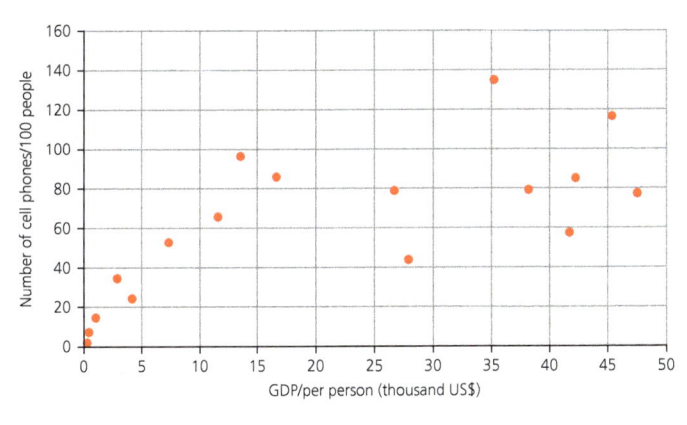

△ Fig. 4.4 How to construct a scatter graph.

- Decide which is your independent variable (in this example, GDP) and which is likely to be the dependent variable (cell phone ownership).
- Plot your axes and decide on a suitable scale for each one. Note that the spaces between values must be the same along each axis.
- Plot the data as you would for a line graph, but do not join the dots:

	GDP/person (US$)	Cell phones per 100 people
UK	45 390	116.6
France	42 250	85.1
etc. ↓		

Best-fit lines

A **best-fit line** can be added to a scatter graph to make it easier to interpret the information that it displays. Best-fit lines are straight; they should also dissect the pattern of dots in the best possible way. In Fig. 4.5 a line has been added to the scatter graph to show how this is done. This line shows that the relationship (link or correlation) between the two plotted data sets is: 'As GDP per person increases, the number of cell phones per 1000 people also increases'.

A best-fit line that rises upwards across a scatter graph is called a **positive correlation**; one that slopes downwards indicates a **negative correlation**. The closer all the dots are to the best-fit line, the stronger the relationship. If all the dots lie exactly along the best-fit line, they show a **'perfect' correlation** between the two sets of data.

Some dots may be so far away from the best-fit line that they don't seem to fit any pattern suggested by the graph. These dots are called **anomalies**. They may also be worth discussing because they are so different to the general pattern.

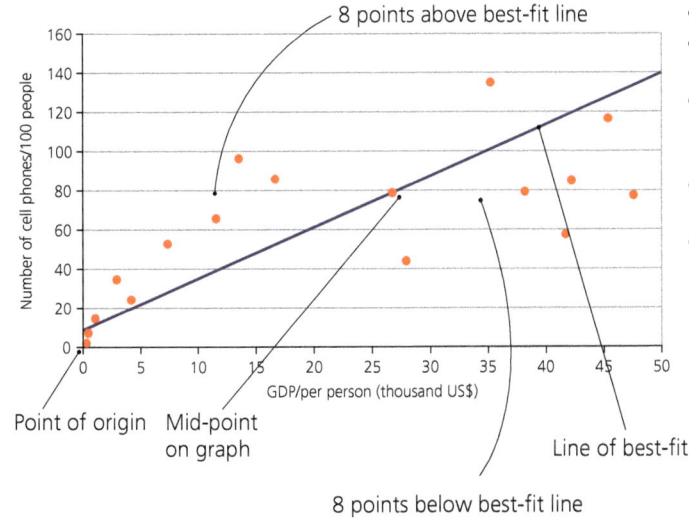

- Identify the mid-point on your graph.
- Place a ruler through this point. (Hint: A clear plastic ruler makes this task easier.)
- Now rotate the ruler around this mid-point until it divides the dots on the graph so that half of them are above it and half below it.
- Draw a pencil line along the ruler's edge: this is your best-fit line.
- There are two key points to remember:
  - the line does not have to pass through the point of origin of the graph
  - while your aim is to split the dots 50:50, it isn't critical if you can't quite do this.

△ Fig. 4.5 How to add a best-fit line to a scatter graph.

Desire line maps

Desire line maps show the *directions* in which people or goods move towards a central place, such as a school or factory. Place names can be added to the end-points of the lines if this is helpful to your enquiry. The length of each line indicates the distance travelled along its direction. A compass point and linear scale must be added to every desire line map.

Flow line maps

Flow line maps show the *volume* of traffic, goods or people along routeways, as well as their direction of movement. The maps need a compass point, as well as a scale, to show what the different flow line thicknesses stand for.

Remote sensing and GIS technology

Remote sensing is the technology of using satellites to obtain images of the Earth's surface. Geographers' real focus is not on how this technology works, but on how the information it provides can be used to explore and explain Earth's mysteries. Maps are probably the geographer's most important tool, and this is why remote sensing is so important. The flow of spatial data from satellites is never-ending, so it constantly updates the information available to us.

GIS stands for **Geographic Information System**, and one of its most important functions is to produce maps from 'layers' of different information types obtained through remote sensing and data capture. One of these layers might display 'physical information' like the height and shape of the land in an area. Another might include some of that area's 'human' features, such as roads and quarries.

Cartographers (map-makers) combine different information-type layers to create the maps needed by different users. Ordnance Survey (OS) maps like that of the Framlingham area in Fig. 4.12 are now based mainly on GIS information, not the time-consuming, open-air surveying techniques of the past.

This background information helps you to appreciate how important GIS maps are to geographers like yourself. The atlases in your classroom become dated very quickly, so it makes sense to search the Internet to find at least one GIS-based map for your enquiry – even if it is as simple as the street layout of a town you are surveying.

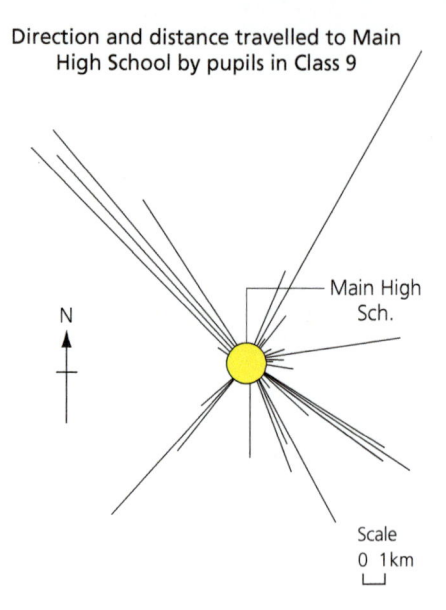

△ Fig. 4.6 A typical desire line map.

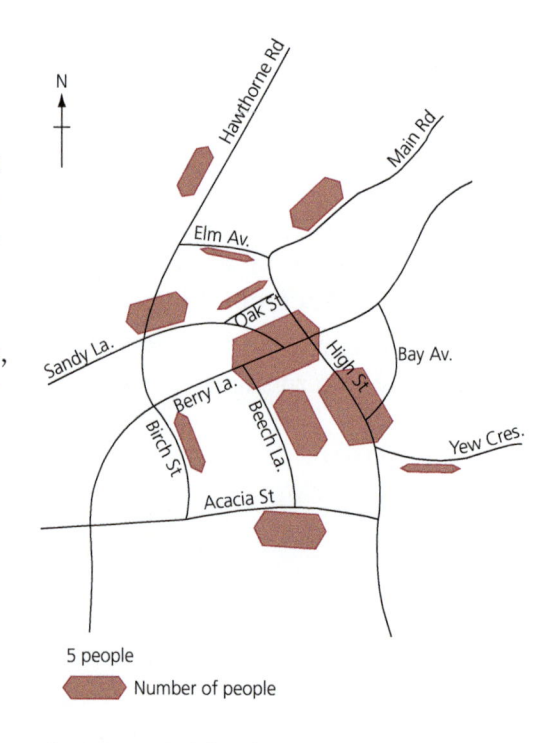

Fig. 4.7 A typical flow line map.

GIS is much more than just maps! GIS systems allow students to enter data directly in the field, and so make full use of hand-held equipment available from school. Electronic equipment is much easier and quicker to use than the traditional data-gathering methods like tape measures and protractors. Such devices will also store the information, which avoids you having to shout it out and someone else trying to write it down, often in poor weather conditions.

Here are some of the things you can do with GIS technology:
- import a range of digital maps
- draw and edit maps and plans by adding your own data
- combine different layers to produce maps that will show all the types of information you need
- zoom in and out of maps at different scales.

Comparing maps

As part of your enquiry, you may need to compare maps of the same area. These can be drawn to different scales and be of different types. You are most likely to come across historical maps, which show what places were like before important developments such as town growth and the building of railways and motorways. Comparing maps with different scales is quite difficult, so it is helpful to enlarge the smaller map until its scale is the same as the larger one.

An OS map extract of the area around Croyde and Woolacombe villages on the north Devon coast is shown in Fig. 4.9. On the facing page is a geology map of the same area, showing the types of bedrock that have helped to shape its coastline. Both maps have exactly the same scale (1:50 000) which makes them easy to compare.

The coastline is clearly this area's most outstanding feature. Some stretches of it jut out into the sea. These are its headlands, called Bull Point, Monte Point and Baggy Point. They are rugged stretches of coast, with rocky shores and steep cliffs. The South West Coast Path follows the line of the coast, so that walkers can enjoy the fine views of these headlands (see Fig. 4.8).

It is likely that the rocks of these headlands are so hard that the sea can't erode them as quickly as the sandy bays between them. Look at the geology map, and you will see that the two headlands are shaded differently to the area between them: the area east of Morte Bay. The map's key identifies the main rock types in each area. The Internet can tell you how hard, and erosion-resistant, each type of rock is. For example Morte Point headland is made of slate, one of the oldest and hardest rocks in the area.

△ Fig. 4.8 The coast around Woolacombe.

△ Fig. 4.9 1:50 000 scale Ordnance Survey map extract of the Woolacombe/Croyde area of the north Devon coast.

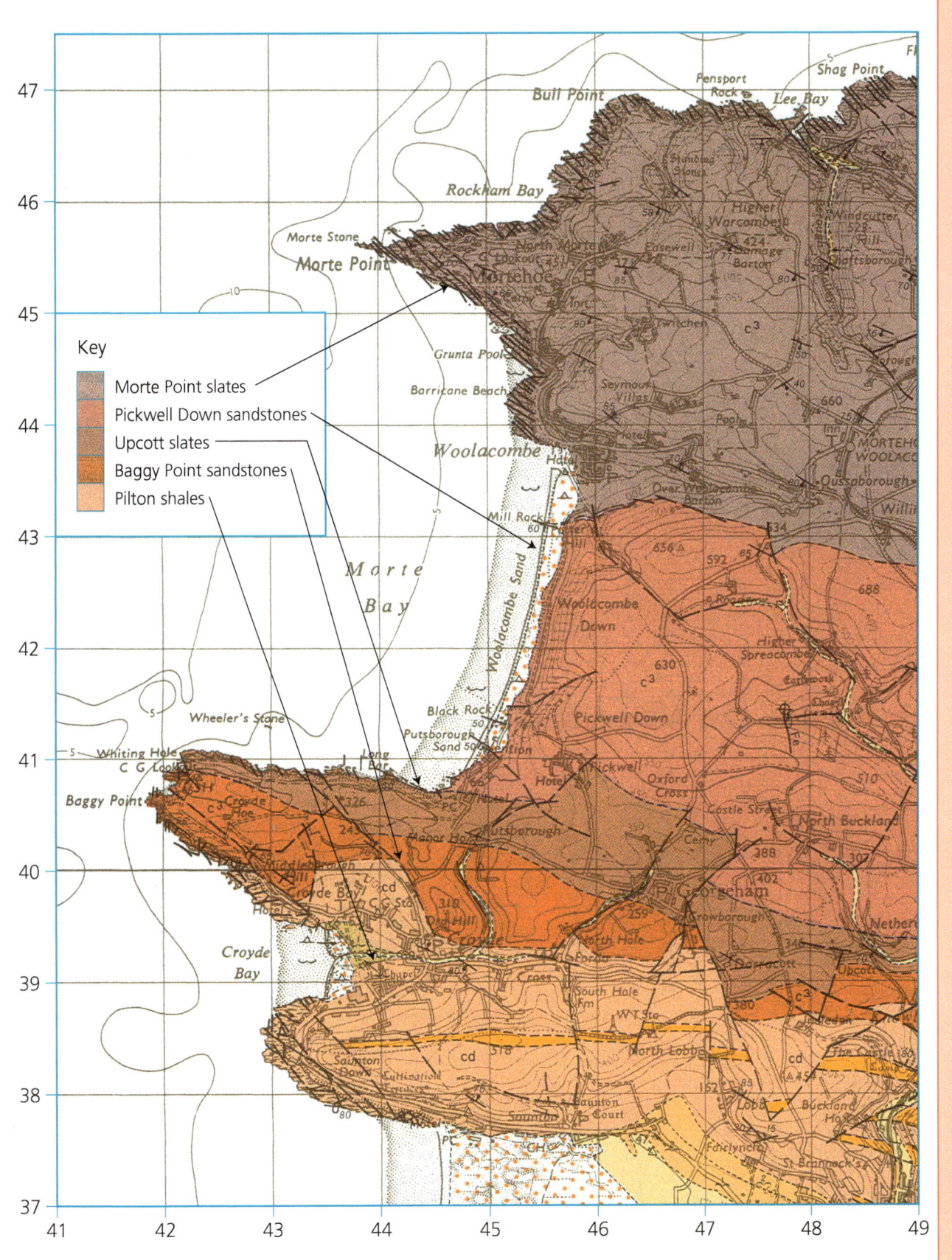

Key
- Morte Point slates
- Pickwell Down sandstones
- Upcott slates
- Baggy Point sandstones
- Pilton shales

△ Fig. 4.10 The geology of the map extract area on the opposite page.

Comparing these two maps (Fig 4.9 and Fig 4.10) shows that the best ways to make map comparisons are:

- Choose maps which have the same scale whenever possible.
- Enlarge or reduce one of the maps to make them both the same scale.
- Look for major features on one of the maps, then study the same places on the other map to see if there are general patterns to suggest links between the two. Both maps' keys will help you to do this.

Describing and explaining map distributions

Every area is different and what information – and *patterns* of information – you want from maps will depend on your enquiry topic. The OS map extract in Fig. 4.12 would be ideal if you wanted to study settlement location and distribution in a rural area. The main settlement on this map is Framlingham, a small town dominated by the huge medieval castle located at GR 286637 (see Fig. 4.11).

Framlingham seems to be at the centre of a ring of villages including Brandeston and Dennington. Look a little more carefully at this pattern, and you will notice that most of them are 4–5 km away from this central market town. The map symbols show that Framlingham has more services than any of these villages, for example a school and a college. It has a post office, which none of the villages have. Other map evidence suggests that settlements have to be a certain size, and a certain distance from larger settlements, to justify them having a church or public house. Even smaller settlements, like the hamlets called Broadwater (grid square 2861) and Saxtead Bottom (square 2665), don't have these basic services.

Another interesting pattern on this map is the routes taken by long distance paths, shown by lines of green dots. You can probably work out for yourself why these routes have been chosen by studying grid squares 2460, 2859, 2863, 2964 and 3166.

△ Fig. 4.11 Framlingham Castle.

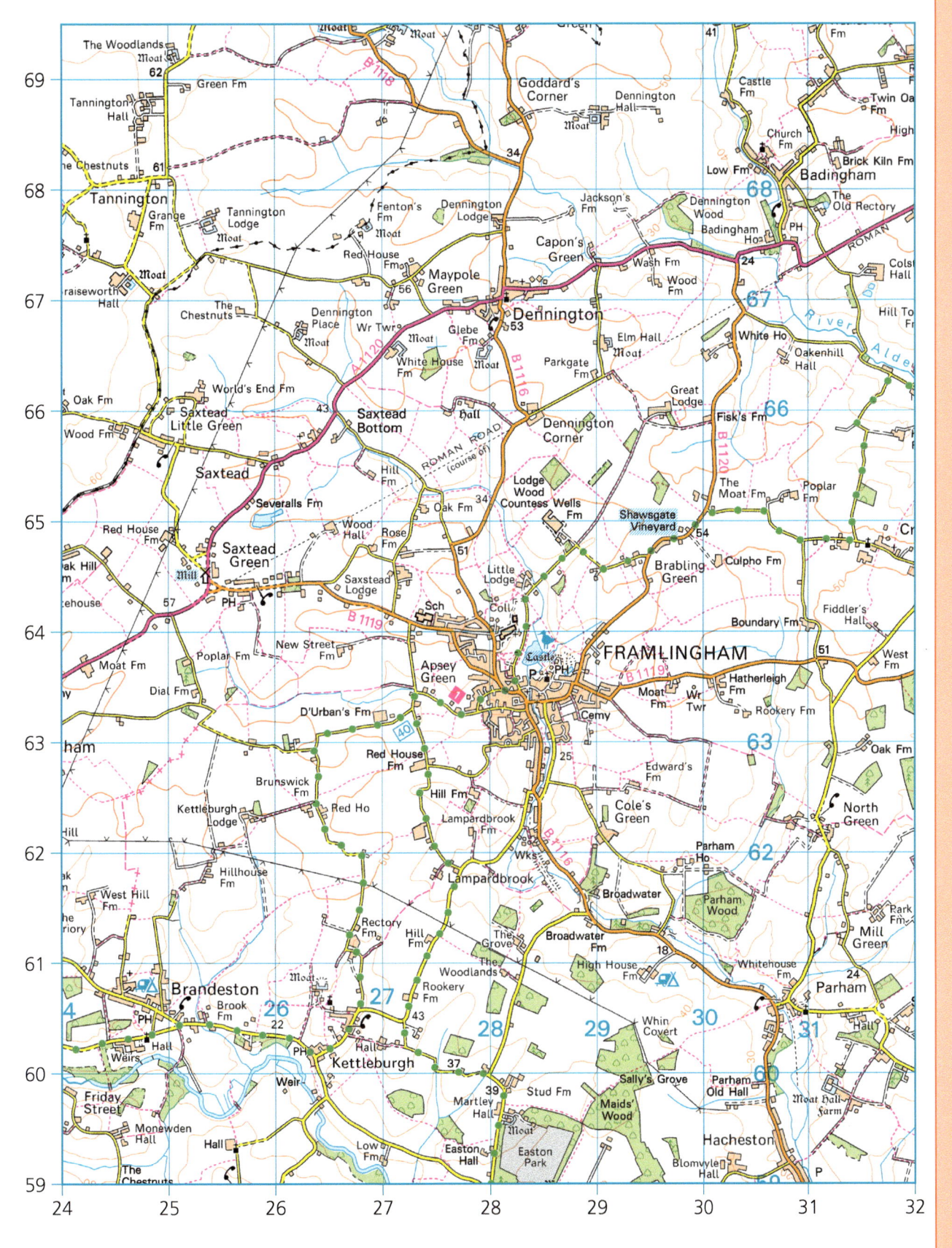

△ Fig. 4.12 1:50 000 scale Ordnance Survey map extract of the Framlingham area in Suffolk.

△ Fig. 4.13 The countryside around Framlingham is an important farming area.

Drawing sketch maps

The easiest way to draw sketch maps is by using good quality tracing paper. You can of course draw your sketch map 'by eye', in which case you will need to follow the guidelines in the flow diagram in Fig. 4.14. Whichever method you choose, remember to include only those map features that are relevant to your enquiry topic.

- Begin with a pencil-drawn frame which is the size of the sketch map you want to produce.

- Add upright and horizontal lines to divide your box into equal-size areas. Draw these lines very faintly because you will be rubbing them out later. The lines are only there to guide you while you are adding features to your map. If what you are sketching is from an OS map, it makes sense for some of your lines to be chosen from some of the blue grid lines on it. For example, on the 1:50 000 scale OS map of the area around Framingham on page 53, you could use every second or fourth line, both horizontally and vertically.

- With the help of the lines on the map and the tracing paper to guide you, draw some of the map's major features such as a coastline, river or the outlines of villages and woods. You can also add any railway lines or major roads at this stage.

- Add any extra information about the map area needed for your enquiry. This can include some of the primary data collected during your outside visits.

- Finally, give your sketch map a title stating where it is located, a compass direction arrow, a linear scale and a symbol/colour shaded key.

△ Fig. 4.14 How to draw a sketch map.

Triangular graphs

Triangular graphs are a way of showing *three* variables on one diagram, each of which must be in percentages, totalling 100 per cent. Their triangular design allows three scales to be used; figure 4.15 shows how information is plotted against each of them. Their scales usually have 10-per-cent intervals.

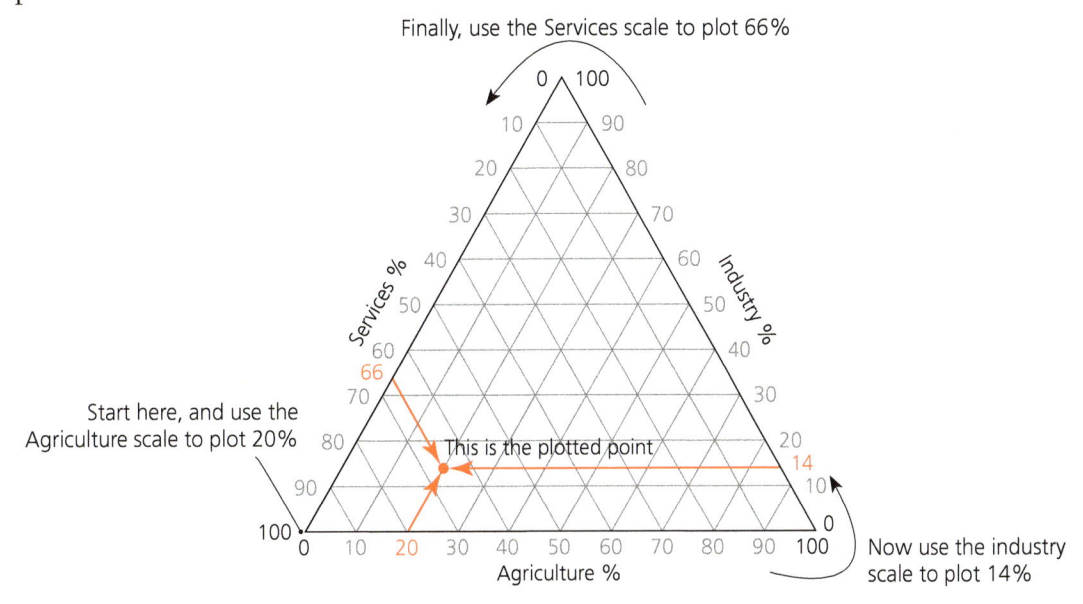

△ Fig. 4.15 How to plot a triangular graph to show the employment structure of an area with 20% agricultural, 14% industrial and 66% service sectors.

Proportional circles

These are circles that are drawn in proportion to the size of the information they represent. To find the length of the radius to draw each circle, simply calculate its square root. It is fine to round each square root to one decimal place, such that 4.57 becomes 4.6 and 8.31 becomes 8.3. Square roots that have 5 as their second decimal place are always rounded *up*, so that 7.85 becomes 7.9.

Proportional circles can just be used to show size. They can also be drawn as pie graphs to increase their usefulness (see page 10–11 for information about how to create these).

Pebble roundness

Pebble roundness is an indicator of several factors, including the speed and frequency of water flow and the hardness of the pebbles themselves. It is therefore a useful activity to include in physical geography enquiries like beach and stream surveys.

△ Fig. 4.16 How to assess pebble roundness.

GCSE fieldwork enquiry components

> **LEARNING OBJECTIVES**
> ✓ Be able to make judgements about the aims, hypotheses and research questions upon which research enquiries are based.
> ✓ Be aware of health and safety issues in a range of environments.
> ✓ Be able to differentiate between primary and secondary sources of data.
> ✓ Be able to understand the skills required to undertake and then evaluate a GCSE geographical enquiry.

Some thoughts before you start…

Your enquiry can be hand-written, or presented using desktop publishing. The decision on how to present it will depend on:

- computer availability in your school
- your family's own computer/laptop/printer availability
- the neatness of your handwriting
- how good your spelling is – using a computer gives you access to a spell-checker, so this might be an important consideration for you
- whether you want to make text corrections neater and easier to do by using desktop publishing.

Here are some other important things to keep in mind:

- **Use key Geography terms whenever you can**. You will be expected to know these, be clear about what they mean, and be able to use them correctly in the examination questions about your fieldwork enquiry. Using them in your write-up is a useful preparation for this. You are also expected to spell these terms correctly, so refer to the Glossary on pages 101–102 or consult a subject directory to check any spellings you are not sure about.
- **Make a record of any problems you experience** when collecting or using data. Do this right away, because it is easy to forget things and you will need to discuss any problems when you are analysing your collected data later on.
- If you decide to use desktop publishing, **save your work frequently** during work sessions. It is both frustrating and time-wasting to have to re-do work, so get into the habit of saving computer work every five minutes, or at the end of each paragraph.
- Also, when using desktop publishing, **keep at least one up-to-date electronic copy of all your work**. To lose an almost complete enquiry is heart-breaking, so avoid this happening at all costs.
- You don't have to spend precious time drawing lots of graphs; it is fine to use downloaded versions of them instead.
- There is no word limit for fieldwork enquiries, so write freely, in whichever style suits you best.

- Avoid using vague words like 'stuff', 'things', 'nice', 'pretty', 'lovely', 'appropriate' and 'OK'! If you do use them, always add some detailed information, for example 'This view is really attractive to people *because*…'.
- Keep your teacher advised of how your enquiry write-up is progressing. It is especially helpful to do this at intervals in the longer, more challenging components that are based on your collected data.

It is also good practice for:

- your **maps** to have a compass direction arrow, a scale and, where necessary, a symbol key
- your **graphs** to have axis labels that indicate the type of information being plotted
- your **illustrations**, such as sketches, photographs and postcards, to be located and have some detailed annotations – using overlays avoids your annotations spoiling the images underneath
- **all writing** for these items to be in ink, not pencil.

The fieldwork enquiry structure

Your finished enquiry should have a structure like that shown in Fig. 5.1, and guidance for completing each component within it is given in the rest of this section. Remember that the enquiry file is your property and

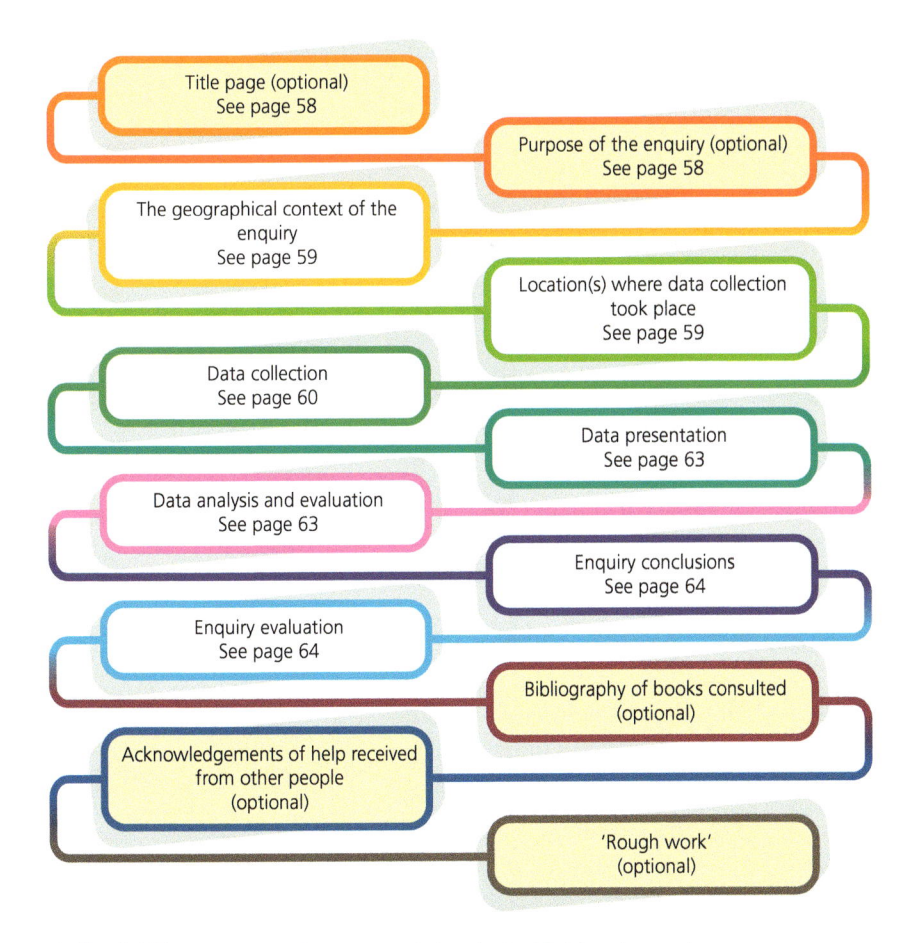

- Title page (optional) See page 58
- Purpose of the enquiry (optional) See page 58
- The geographical context of the enquiry See page 59
- Location(s) where data collection took place See page 59
- Data collection See page 60
- Data presentation See page 63
- Data analysis and evaluation See page 63
- Enquiry conclusions See page 64
- Enquiry evaluation See page 64
- Bibliography of books consulted (optional)
- Acknowledgements of help received from other people (optional)
- 'Rough work' (optional)

△ Fig. 5.1 The sequence of components in a typical fieldwork enquiry.

you might like to keep it as a memento of your visits out of school with your friends. You should certainly keep it safe if you are thinking of studying Geography at AS, A or degree level.

The title page (optional)
You should include a brief title, which identifies both the enquiry topic and its main location(s). You also need to include your name and the name of your school. Try to make this first page look attractive, because it sets the standard of presentation for the important enquiry components that follow. If space allows, you could also add some illustrations, such as postcards bought during your visit, to make your title page more interesting.

A contents page (optional)
It is up to you whether or not to include a contents page showing the sequence of your enquiry components. It is probably best to leave this to the very end – when you know exactly what has been put into your file.

The purpose of the enquiry
Each GCSE Geography specification gives schools some choice in what fieldwork topics they may investigate. These are usually closely linked to the topics that are taught in preparation for the Year 11 examinations. However, most schools like their teachers to be closely involved in the selection of enquiry aims. This is because they need to consider factors like:

- health and safety issues, and the number of staff needed to supervise students
- the availability of suitable transport
- the amount, type and reliability of available equipment
- the cost implications of visits for the school and students' families.

Students may be allowed some input in drafting the wording of research questions, and doing this certainly gives them more 'ownership' of the enquiry process.

There are three ways of stating the purpose of a geographical enquiry. These are listed below.

Aims – These are *intentions*. They state what the enquiry is designed to investigate.

Two examples of enquiry aims are:
- 'To investigate the ways in which brownfield sites have been redeveloped in (*name of town*).'
- 'To compare the range of services provided in villages with different populations.'

Hypotheses – These are *statements*, which the enquiry process is designed to prove or disprove. It may do neither, which is a third and equally valid outcome!

Two examples of enquiry hypotheses are:

- 'Bus routes always follow the main roads of a town.'
- 'That the water is always shallower close to the inner bends of stream meanders.'

Starting a hypothesis with *'That'* is entirely optional.

Research questions – These are *questions* which, when answered, should achieve the purpose of the enquiry.

Two examples of enquiry questions are:

- 'Should more traffic calming measures be installed in the Central Business District of (*name of town*)?'
- 'How effective are the coastal management strategies designed to protect (*name of place*)?'

It is up to you to decide whether to use just one aim, hypothesis or question. Sometimes, it is useful to have a combination of the three, for example by having one major aim (or hypothesis), followed by three or four questions. Questions help to structure an enquiry and make it easier to reach final conclusions.

It is good practice to explain why you thought your chosen research topic would be interesting to investigate, as well as relevant to your Geography course.

The geographical context of the enquiry

Every enquiry can be linked to some form of geographical knowledge or theory. Textbooks and the Internet provide background information that can put your enquiry in a geographical context. For example, if you planned to survey the flow characteristics of a local stream, it would be helpful to discover what your textbook, borrowed library books and Internet sites have to say on the subject. You will find that they tend to suggest the same: that the current usually swings towards the outer bank of a meander and this is why it has eroded more quickly and become steeper than an inner bank. Finding and then using contextual information like this is *not* cheating! In fact, it provides a very 'professional' start to an enquiry.

Location(s) where data collection took place

Make it clear where your enquiry activities were undertaken. Using maps of different scales allows you to locate your activities in several ways:

- Its *national* location – by using a latitude and longitude position from an atlas map.

- Its *regional* location – by using an atlas or GIS map. Google Earth and Multimap provide maps suitable for locating enquiries.
- Its *neighbourhood* location – by using four- or six-figure grid reference locations on a 1:50 000 or 1:25 000 scale map.
- Its *precise* location (if necessary) – by using larger-scale OS maps or detailed street plans.

Every location map needs to include a compass direction arrow, a scale and the exact location(s) of the enquiry. There should also be some written description of these location(s) as shown by your maps. This could name:

- the geographical area the enquiry is to take place in
- nearby settlements such as conurbations, towns and villages, and add their compass directions and direct distances
- any significant areas of high or low land
- (if relevant) the river and sea into which a stream eventually flows.

You also need to write briefly about what your enquiry location is like. This will depend on whether your enquiry is about a 'human' or a 'physical' geography topic. For example, a study based on an urban area should include some background information about that settlement, such as:

- a brief description of its original site, and the main advantages of that place for establishing a new settlement
- how and why it developed over time, highlighting any major events influencing its growth, such as the Industrial Revolution of 1760–1850
- a statement of its present size, population and economic functions.

Some of this information could be displayed very effectively as a timeline.

Data collection

This can be an enjoyable part of your enquiry, because it is quite easy to do and can bring back memories of your visits out of school. Points to consider when writing this section are:

- Identify and briefly describe each method you used to collect the data.
- If possible, include photographs or diagrams of the equipment you used; these can easily be downloaded from the Internet if the pictures taken on the day prove disappointing.
- Explain *how* the equipment was used to collect data.
- Describe 'who did what' in the data collection process. It is best if everyone in your group contributed actively to the collection and took turns at performing each role.
- Note down briefly any advantages – and disadvantages – of using each piece of equipment and data collection method.
- Write down the timings of the data collection (if relevant). For example, the volume of traffic on a main road will be much heavier in rush hour periods than at any other time of the day. You will need to refer to information like this later on, when writing the evaluation section of your enquiry.

- It is often impossible to collect all the data you would wish to in the time allowed. This means that you will need to use some form of sampling. For example, if you were measuring the height of groynes above the level of beach material, it would be appropriate to use alternate groynes instead of every single one.
- A data set that has fewer than 20 items is often considered too small to be reliable, so always aim for more than this if possible.
- Remember that it is helpful to obtain data sets in multiples of 20, because these figures are easy to convert into percentages for plotting divided bar graphs, and degrees for use with pie charts.
- This may be obvious, but *don't* include irrelevant information like who was driving the school's minibus! Instead, focus on how the data was actually collected.

The primary data you collected will probably be your enquiry's most import information. Secondary data is also important; so important that your GCSE specification will probably require you to include some. The spider diagram in Fig. 5.2 shows some of the many secondary data sources that can be accessed by students in school or at home. During outside visits, take some time out to buy any postcards, maps and newspapers that might provide useful local information.

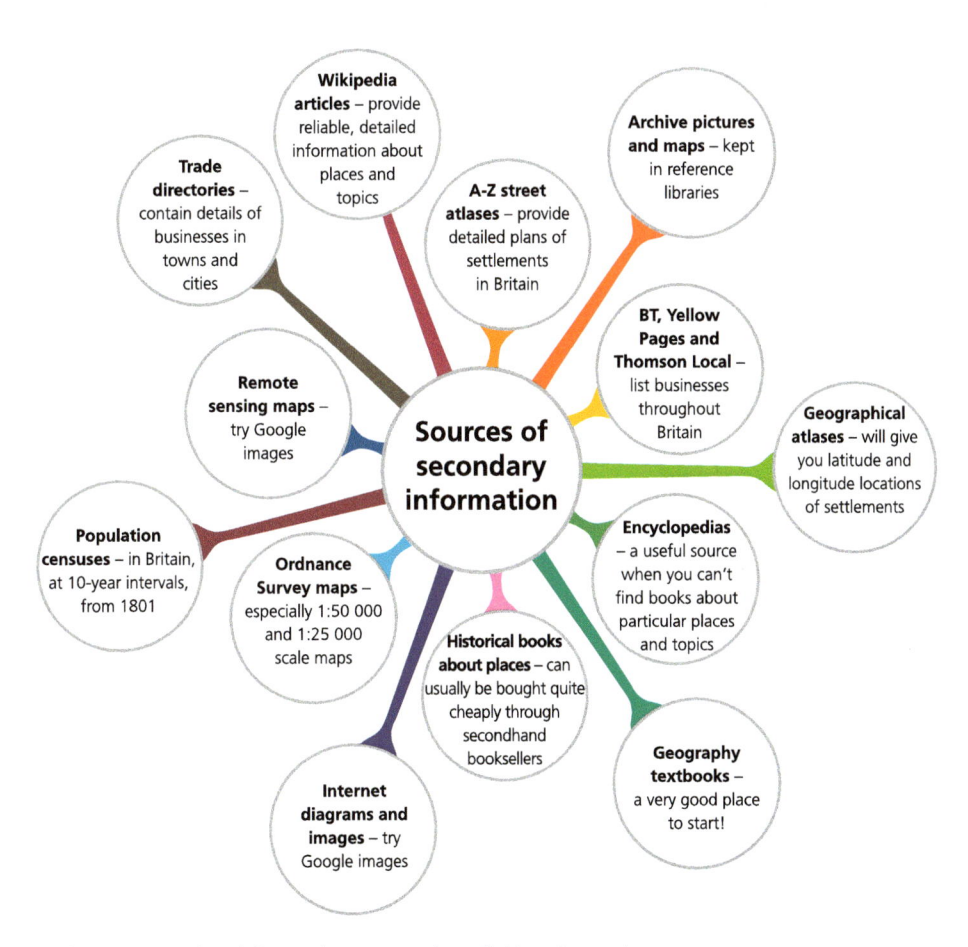

△ Fig. 5.2 Secondary information sources for a fieldwork enquiry.

WATCH OUT

Health and safety issues

Health and safety issues are important, and careful thought will have been given to them when planning your fieldwork trip. These issues will depend on the location and type of data being collected. For example, you are likely to meet some very different issues while carrying out a traffic census than you would collecting stream-flow data. A good way of highlighting likely issues is to summarise them in a table like the one on page 75, used for a land use transect in Rochdale.

It is unusual for everything to run perfectly smoothly on outside visits. This is because fieldwork activities depend on so many factors: the students taking part, the people they meet, transport arrangements, the correct functioning of data collection equipment and, of course, the weather!

A common issue is avoiding repeat interviews with the same people. These are time-wasting for students and annoying to the public. It obviously isn't possible to rubber-stamp people when they have been interviewed, but some advance thought should be given to reducing foreseeable problems like this. Some of the more likely hazards in four popular data collection environments are listed below.

On a busy street

- Lots of traffic, including heavy goods vehicles and buses.
- Cyclists weaving about on roads and pavements.
- Pavements crowded with pedestrians, forcing students onto the road.
- Muggers, pick-pockets and other anti-social people.

On the edge of a village

- Herds of cows crossing the road.
- Animal droppings on the road.
- Farmers' dogs (some students are very scared of dogs).
- Angry bulls.
- Animals escaping through field gates left open.
- Tractors towing trailers and other large farm machinery, causing traffic jams on narrow roads.
- Winding roads making it difficult to see oncoming traffic.

On a beach

- Rock armour boulders often have jagged edges.
- Slimy weeds on wooden groynes are very slippery.
- Waves crashing on the shore.
- Family groups wanting privacy while bathing.
- Students unable to swim are at risk of drowning.
- Dog droppings and other unpleasant waste.
- Unsuitable footwear for beach and groyne surveys.
- Risk of sunburn.

Around a stream

- Slippery rock surfaces.
- Boggy, marshy areas on banks and paths leading down to a stream.
- Fast-flowing water.

- Pockets of deeper water that are difficult to see.
- Fishermen's fly-hooks.
- Losing equipment, particularly expensive electronic data-recording devices.
- Unsuitable footwear for stream and bank surveys.
- Risk of sunburn.

Data presentation

This part of your enquiry displays the information that has been collated back at school. It is up to you to decide which presentation methods to use, but here are some words of advice.

- Use a range of different methods, instead of restricting yourself to just one or two.
- It is fine to use computer-generated diagrams, but also good practice to draw a few of them yourself.
- Use the most appropriate method for displaying each type of data. For example, you should use a divided bar graph or pie graph for data that is broken down into parts, like the number of road vehicles of different types in a traffic census.
- Give each diagram an appropriate title.
- Add a colour key, if necessary.
- Always write titles, labels and other text elements in ink.
- When you use illustrations like photographs and sketches, don't just stick them in as 'pretty pictures'. Instead, annotate them so that they are more useful when you come to write your conclusions.
- Briefly describe the data displayed in each diagram. Record any general patterns in the data, as well as anomalies that don't fit these.
- Don't include any explanations for what your items show; these belong in the next section.
- You can include in this section the tables that provide data for your diagrams. However, there will probably be several of these, so you might prefer to group them together in a separate 'Rough Work' appendix to your enquiry.

Data analysis and evaluation

This can be the most challenging section – because it is where you try to make sense of all the information your group has collected. This includes suggesting reasons for any information patterns and anomalies that you identified in the last section.

While doing this, you should always have in mind the aims, hypotheses or questions that your enquiry is investigating. One way of approaching this task is to write each of these on separate sheets of lined paper. You can then make notes under each heading as you go carefully back through your completed data presentation and evaluation components. When you've done all this, it should be a fairly easy task to write a mini-conclusion at the bottom of each sheet.

You may get 'writer's block' in this section – this is when you can't write down what you want to say, because the right words simply won't come to mind. If this happens to you, and it almost certainly will at some point, try 'talking' through the topic in your head; playing with different combinations of words until you get close to what you want to say. Then write them down quickly, because you can always return to them later and refine the wording until it is exactly right.

Enquiry conclusions

You have now reached the last important stage of your enquiry. This is where you bring together all your mini-conclusions to produce one clear, final conclusion that is based on the data you have collected, presented and evaluated.

- If your main target was to test a **hypothesis**, you will need to say whether it was proved, disproved or neither. If it is 'neither', suggest possible reasons for this – with your teacher's help, if necessary.
- If it was an **aim**, write a summary of what you have discovered in order to meet it.
- If it was a **question**, simply answer it!

This is also where you should assess how closely your findings compare with the model (or other subject knowledge) that you considered when first deciding what to investigate.

Enquiry evaluation

Part of the evaluation process is to reflect on what went particularly well – or badly – during your data collection. As you do this, focus on the methods used rather than the people who were using them. Doing this will help you to avoid unhelpful responses like:

- 'We should have worked much harder to get the work done.'
- 'There simply wasn't enough time to do everything.'
- 'The weather didn't help us one bit!'

If you believe that any of your problems were really serious, explain how they made it difficult to collect enough quality data. You might also suggest how they might be avoided in a future, similar enquiry. You may need your teacher's help to do this.

Also, if you now think that the wording of any of your hypotheses, aims or questions could have been improved, this is the place to say so – and to suggest an alternative wording.

Bibliography of books consulted (optional)

This can be as simple as a list of book titles, their authors and publishers.

Acknowledgements of help received from other people (optional)

You may wish to thank any teachers or librarians who have been of help. It might also be appropriate to acknowledge the willingness of local people to be interviewed or provide other information.

'Rough work' (optional)

This can include the first drafts of your text, rough sketches and completed interview questionnaires.

Suggested GCSE fieldwork enquiries

Enquiry 1: The Central Business District
Aim: to locate and investigate a town's Central Business District.

QUESTIONS

1. Where is the CBD located, in relation to the whole of the town?
2. Is this the original site, and was it a suitable place to establish a town?
3. What are the main buildings in the CBD, and what are their functions?
4. Do some parts of the CBD/streets in it specialise in certain functions?

Geographical context
The CBD is the 'heart' of a town. It is usually located at its original site, and where the main roads meet, but may not actually be at its centre! The CBDs of ports and coastal holiday resorts are often next to the shore.

The CBD is multi-functional. Its four main roles are:

- **Commercial:** hotels, major shops, specialist shops, banks, offices.
- **Public buildings:** town hall, library, museum, police station, job centre.
- **Recreational:** theatres, nightclubs, pubs, restaurants.
- **Transport:** railway station, bus station, multi-storey car parks, taxi ranks.

Location identification resources
- Map to locate the town chosen for the enquiry within its region.
- OS maps that include the town's urban area.

WATCH OUT
Main health and safety issues

- Work in small groups – never alone.
- Know where your teachers and their transport are located.
- Always carry a reliable mobile phone in case of emergencies.
- Stay on pavements – well away from road traffic.
- Beware of pick-pockets, muggers and gangs.

Data collection activities
- Complete (or update) a land use plan of the CBD.
- Identify any 'specialist' areas or streets within the CBD.
- Locate the outer edge of the CBD zone.

Data collection equipment required
Street/building plan of central area likely to contain the CBD, a code system for recording different building uses, cameras, clipboards, pencils and wet-weather protection for survey sheets.

Suggested sources of secondary data
- Internet site and reference libraries providing information about the original site of the town and its development up to the present time.
- Goad street plan. This will show the ground-floor use of every building at the time of its survey. (**Note:** Goad plans are only produced for towns with populations over 50 000).
- Visitors' town map available from local Tourist Information Centre.

Recommended data presentation and analysis
- Maps to locate the survey town and its CBD area.
- Street plan to locate any specialist areas/streets within it.
- Goad plan map (or equivalent) to plot individual building usage.
- Undertake nearest neighbour analysis, such as for hotels, banks, estate agents, large shops, solicitors, charity shops, restaurants/cafes.

Enquiry 2: Soil depth and pH patterns across fields
Aim: to investigate whether soil depth and pH are linked to factors such as the slope of the land and different farming activities.

QUESTIONS

1. How are soil depth and pH linked to the downward slope of a field?
2. How are soil depth and pH linked to land relief across a field?

Geographical context
There are many reasons why soil depth can change within a field. These include erosion, rainwater flow over the surface, wind blowing over dry ground, the grazing of animals, the ploughing of arable fields and foot erosion caused by walkers.

Soil pH is also linked to many factors. These include rainwater leaching, the presence of animals and applications such as fertilisers.

Location identification resources
- Locate the farm where the survey is to take place.
- Locate the surveyed fields within the farm.
- Locate any public paths or bridleways that cross or border these fields.
- Summarise the farmer's use of these fields in recent years.

WATCH OUT

Main health and safety issues
- Walk around the fields in pairs or groups – never alone.
- Know where your teachers and their transport are located.
- Always carry a reliable mobile phone in case of emergencies.
- Avoid contact with growing crops, dogs, other farm animals and ponds.
- Avoid treading on animal waste in the fields and on lanes.

Data collection activities
- Obtaining maps, plans and images of the farm and its surrounding area. Include GIS images in your search.
- Making a record of recent rainfall trends in the local area.
- Taking and recording soil depth and pH measurements.

Data collection equipment
- Clipboards, pencils and wet-weather protection for clipboards.
- Cameras – to record the layout and usage of the surveyed fields.
- Graduated prods – to measure soil depth, plus wipes to stop the prods becoming clogged with soil.
- Ranging poles, tape measures and clinometers to obtain field size and gradients.
- Soil testing kits.

Sources of secondary data
- Maps to locate the farm.
- Plan of the farm's fields.
- Internet data on recent local rainfall trends and the soil depth and pH tolerances of individual crops.

Data presentation and analysis
- Maps to locate the farm.
- Farm plan – to locate, identify and measure the survey fields.
- Relief cross-sections, both down and across the surveyed fields, with lines of soil depth and pH readings added to them.
- Line graphs to plot changing soil depth and pH along survey transects.
- Correlation strengths between sets of collected data.

Enquiry 3: Quality of life in rural areas

Aim: to investigate changes in the quality of life in a rural area.

QUESTIONS

1. What community amenities are currently available in villages?
2. What changes to their amenities have taken place in the last five years?
3. How have these villages' populations changed in recent years?
4. Would people prefer to continue living in these villages, or live elsewhere – and why?

Geographical context

Some of the many recent changes to village life and amenities are:

- The closure of schools, shops, post offices, banks, surgeries, garages and village halls.
- Churches have become part of 'clusters', with several villages sharing one minister.
- Bus services have been cancelled, or are much less frequent.
- Farming has become more mechanised, so needs fewer workers.
- Many houses have become second homes, and local people can no longer afford to buy their own property.
- Most newcomers commute elsewhere, so villages are 'empty' for much of a working day.

Location identification resources

- Regional map to locate the survey area.
- OS maps to locate villages included in the survey.

WATCH OUT

Main health and safety issues

- Interview in pairs or threes – never alone.
- Know where your teachers and their transport are located.
- Always carry a reliable mobile phone in case of emergencies.
- Stay out of farmers' fields, and avoid contact with farm animals, growing crops, dogs and ponds.
- Avoid treading on animal waste on the lanes.

Data collection activities

The main source of primary data will be questionnaire-based interviews. Their purpose is to provide information that will help to answer the enquiry's four research questions.

Data collection equipment required
Questionnaires, cameras, clipboards, pencils and wet-weather protection for clipboards.

Suggested sources of secondary data
- Internet sites and OS maps to obtain information about village amenities.
- Wikipedia, to obtain village populations.
- Remote sensing aerial and Streetview images, to obtain up-to-date information about the villages in the survey.

Recommended data presentation and evaluation
- Maps to locate the survey area and individual villages within it.
- A range of graph types to display information collated from the interviews.
- Fact-files, annotated sketches and photographs to record village features such as amenities and new housing.

Enquiry 4: Stream meander characteristics
Aim: to investigate stream meander characteristics.

QUESTIONS

1. How does water depth change across a meander?
2. How does a stream's speed of flow change across a meander?
3. How does a stream's bed load change across a meander?
4. How do a meander's opposite banks differ from each other?

Geographical context
Most meanders display the following characteristics: towards the outer bank, the water is deeper, faster flowing and has a heavier load, with larger, more rounded pebbles. The outer bank is usually steeper and forms a river cliff; the inner bank (the slip-off slope) has a gentler gradient.

Location identification resources
- Maps to locate the river.
- Larger-scale maps to plot the course of the river and locate the survey points along it.

WATCH OUT

Main health and safety issues

- Be aware of faster-flowing water, hidden deeper pools, slippery stones and marshy river banks.
- Make sure that there is a confident swimmer in each group.
- Always obtain data by working in pairs or groups – never alone.
- Know where your teachers and their transport are located.
- Always carry a reliable mobile phone in case of emergencies.

Data collection activities across each meander

- Measuring water depth.
- Measuring the speed of water flow.
- Recording the size and roundness of pebble samples.
- Measuring the height and gradient of each opposite bank.

Data collection equipment required

- Graduated stick to measure water depth.
- Flow meters or stop watches and floats to measure water speed.
- Callipers and Power's Index to measure pebble size and roundness.
- Tape measures, ranging poles and clinometers to measure bank height and gradient.
- Cameras to record stream features and pebble clusters.

Suggested sources of secondary data

- Geography textbooks to increase students' knowledge of meander characteristics.
- GIS images of the surveyed stretches of stream.

Recommended data presentation and analysis

- Cross-section diagrams to record stream width, stream depth, water speed and bank height and gradient across each meander.
- Bar graphs to record pebble size and roundness.
- Scatter graphs and best-fit lines to investigate links between recorded data sets.
- Annotated sketches and photographs to record data collection methods and stream features.

More suggested enquiries available at www.collins.co.uk/FWGCSEGeo

Urban model GCSE enquiry: Rochdale

A model human geography fieldwork enquiry examining Rochdale by a GCSE student

LEARNING OBJECTIVE

✓ To be able to complete a human geography fieldwork enquiry to a high standard.

Hypothesis: That Rochdale's town structure is typical of UK industrial settlements.

QUESTIONS

1. Does Rochdale have a Central Business District, with land uses that are less common than in its other zones?
2. Do Rochdale's industry and housing concentrate in certain parts of the town?
3. Is Rochdale's outer zone a typical rural–urban fringe area?

The geographical context

In our geography Key Stage 3 lessons, we learned that many UK towns have a structure like the one in this diagram. All our towns are different, of course, because they are built in different kinds of physical landscapes. At first glance, it looks as though Rochdale could have this kind of structure. The purpose of this enquiry is to see how true this is, by surveying a transect between its centre and its outer edge.

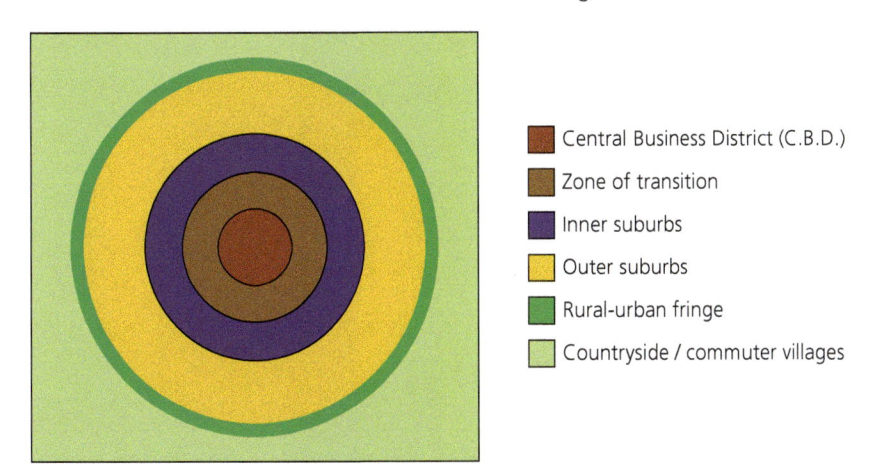

- Central Business District (C.B.D.)
- Zone of transition
- Inner suburbs
- Outer suburbs
- Rural-urban fringe
- Countryside / commuter villages

The historical context

Rochdale is a very ancient settlement, and it even featured in the famous Domesday Book of 1086! Much later, it became an important centre for the woollen trade in the north of England. Later still, cotton replaced wool as its main trade. Rochdale's population grew very rapidly during the Industrial Revolution of 1780–1850. It specialised in cotton spinning. However, its textile and engineering industries declined during the late twentieth century, mainly due to cheaper imports from abroad. Its main function now is to act as a dormitory town for people who commute daily to work in other, more prosperous, places like Manchester.

The locations where we collected our data

Rochdale is part of the Greater Manchester metropolitan area – one of the largest conurbations in northern England. It takes its name from the River Roch, which has its tributaries in the foothills of the South Pennines, and later flows into the River Irwell, then the River Mersey and finally the Irish Sea. It lies 16 km north-northeast of Manchester, and its biggest near neighbour is Oldham, 8.5 km to the southeast.

The first map shows Rochdale's situation in northern England, and its latitude and longitude position: 53° 36' N, 2° 10' W.

The second map is a 1:50 000 scale Ordnance Survey map extract. Its area extends from the town centre, southwards to the boundary with Oldham. It includes the starting and finishing points of the 3.5-km long transect chosen for this enquiry: GR912093 and GR897134 respectively.

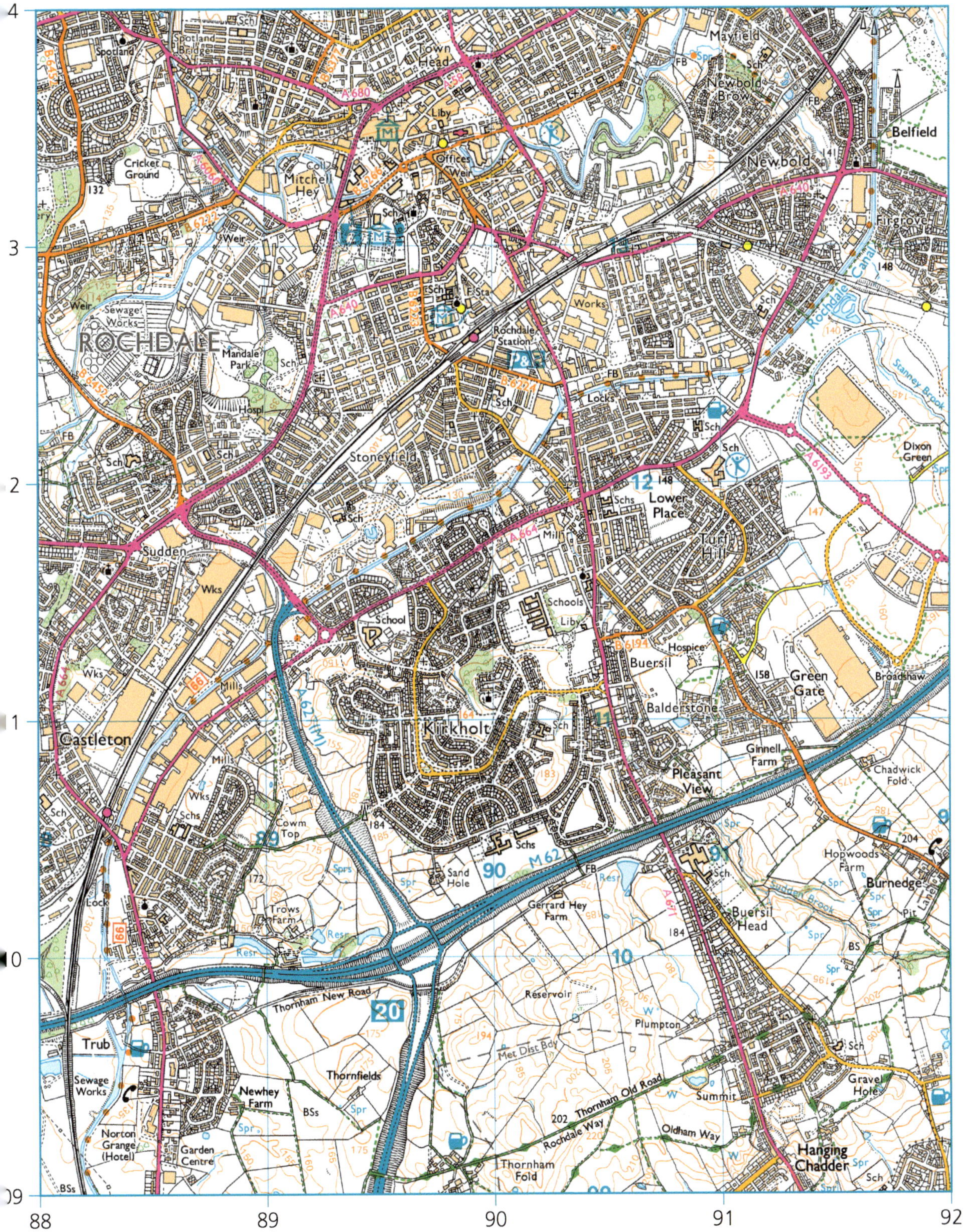

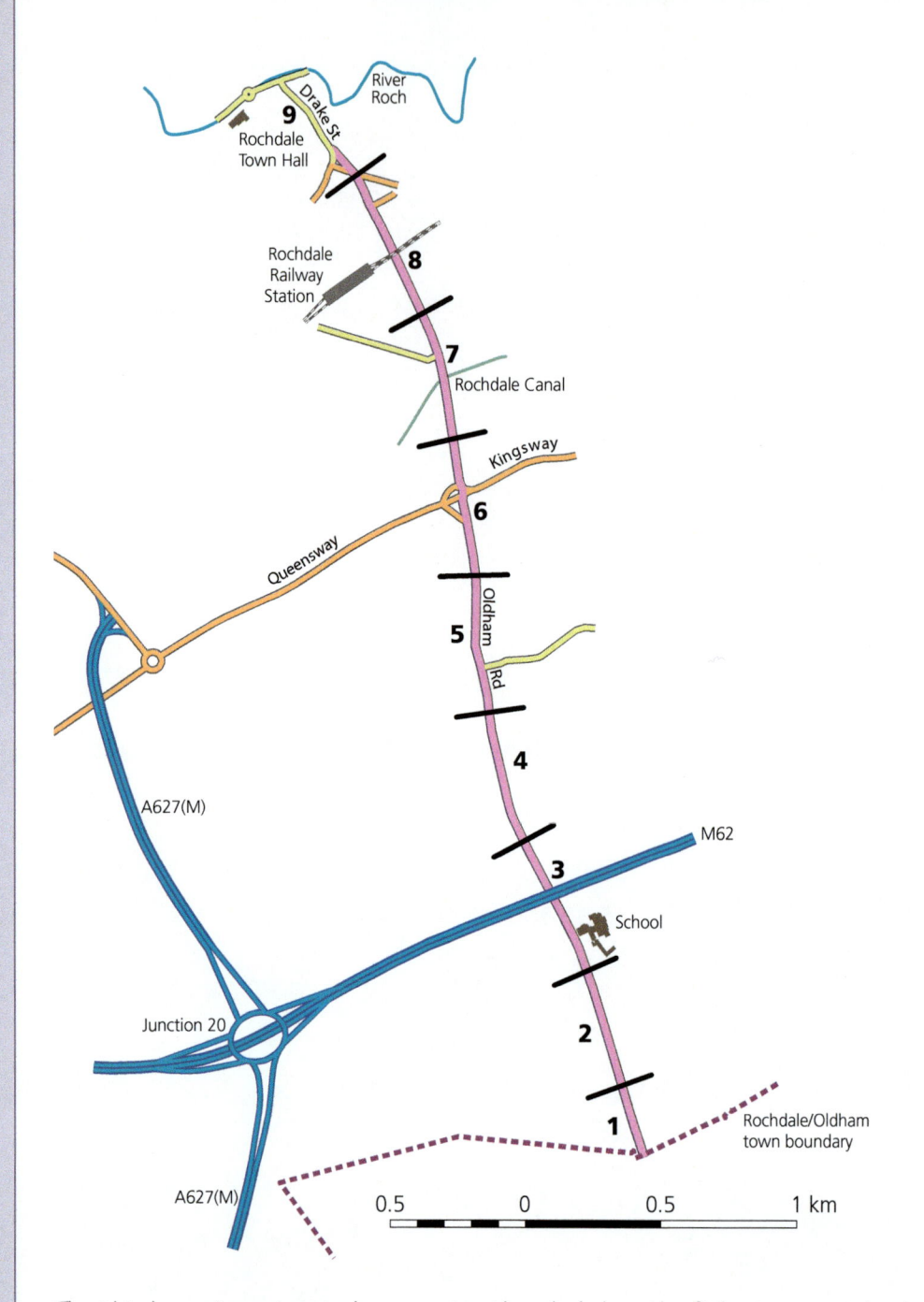

The third map is a street plan covering the whole length of the transect. It shows its final section, the northern part of Drake Street, and the much longer section along Oldham Road, the A671. For the purpose of this enquiry, the transect is divided up into nine survey sections, each of roughly the same length.

Health and safety issues

Drake Street and Oldham Road are both busy routeways and pass through some very different areas of the town. These include areas of derelict land, abandoned industrial premises and run-down housing. Because of this, we were given this sheet of possible health and safety issues, as well as advice on what to do if problems occurred while we are collecting data for our enquiry.

RISK ASSESSMENT FOR COLLECTING FIELDWORK DATA IN AN URBAN AREA

TYPE OF RISK	WHERE/HOW RISK IS MOST LIKELY TO HAPPEN	ACTION TO BE TAKEN TO REDUCE THIS RISK
Road traffic	Being knocked down by passing traffic.	Keep off roads – except when crossing them on pedestrian crossings and the green 'OK to cross' light is on. Don't run straight out onto the road to rescue equipment or a hat which has blown off. Don't avoid groups of pedestrians on the pavement by running around them off the kerb and onto the roadside. Don't walk too close to the pavement kerb – you could be hit by side mirrors on large passing vehicles.
Trips / falls	Many pavements are uneven – especially if they are flagged, cobbled or have ruts in them. Shoes can catch on manhole covers.	Keep a lookout ahead for uneven surfaces. Wear 'sensible' footwear, not high-heeled shoes.
Bicycles	Cyclists riding on pavement. Walking on designated cycle tracks.	Keep a lookout for cyclists weaving about between pedestrians on pavements. Cyclists have priority on cycle tracks, so keep off the tracks because cyclists will ride much faster on them.
Getting lost	This is easy to do when you are collecting data and talking to other students.	Don't lose your street plan! Watch out for helpful road signs like 'To the Town Centre'. Make sure your mobile phone battery is fully charged and the phone has credit on it. Know who to phone for advice. Know where your teachers and transport are during the day.
Street crime	Mugging, theft, unpleasantness.	Stay in your group – don't wander off by yourself. Keep your mobile phone and other 'attractive' items hidden.
Weather	Sunburn, getting very cold and wet.	If bright sunlight is likely, have sun-block cream handy. Be appropriately dressed for the time of year. Keep some spare clothing in a rucksack.

Data collection

We divided the 3.5-km transect route into nine sections, each of them about the same length. For each section, we kept a record of how many units there were in the land use categories we had agreed to use. Back in school, we had decided that:

- Terraced houses and flats would be in the same category.
- Detached and semi-detached houses would also be in the same category.
- 'Old' and 'new' industrial units would be in just one category.

Data presentation

The land use information we collected is displayed in this table.

Individual land use	% for S1	% for S2	% for S3	% for S4	% for S5	% for S6	% for S7	% for S8	% for S9
Terraced housing & flats	44		66	32	70	42	19	3	
Detached & semi-detached housing	54	98	3	48					
Shops & commerce	2		8	4	13	53	42	67	78
Entertainment & services			5	3	6	4	1	6	12
Industry		2	3				25	13	
Public buildings			3	2	3	1	1		3
Derelict and other open land			12	11	8		12	11	7
TOTALS	100	100	100	100	100	100	100	100	100

Back at school, some of the percentages in the first table were combined to make them easier to plot and then analyse. This second table is the result. Its cells have been highlighted in different colours to show which land uses dominate each transect section.

Sector land use	% for S1	% for S2	% for S3	% for S4	% for S5	% for S6	% for S7	% for S8	% for S9	Mean % for all sections
Housing	98	98	69	80	70	42	19	3		53.2
Shops & commerce	2		8	4	13	53	42	67	78	29.7
Services & entertainment			5	3	6	4	1	6	12	4.1
Industry		2	3				25	13		4.8
Public buildings			3	2	3	1	1		3	1.4
Derelict and other open land			12	11	8		12	11	7	6.8
TOTALS	100	100	100	100	100	100	100	100	100	100.0

Section 1 Although this first section has a mix of terraced and detached/semi-detached dwellings, the overall quality of its housing is very high. Some of the detached houses are very impressive, with large gardens. The terraces are built of red brick and date from the Victorian period – probably from when there was a small hill-top village here. This has since expanded due to its attractive semi-rural location and nearby Tandle Hill Country Park on the west side of the road. There are two shops to meet the day-to-day needs of the local people, most of whom are likely to be commuters who work in Rochdale, Oldham or Manchester.

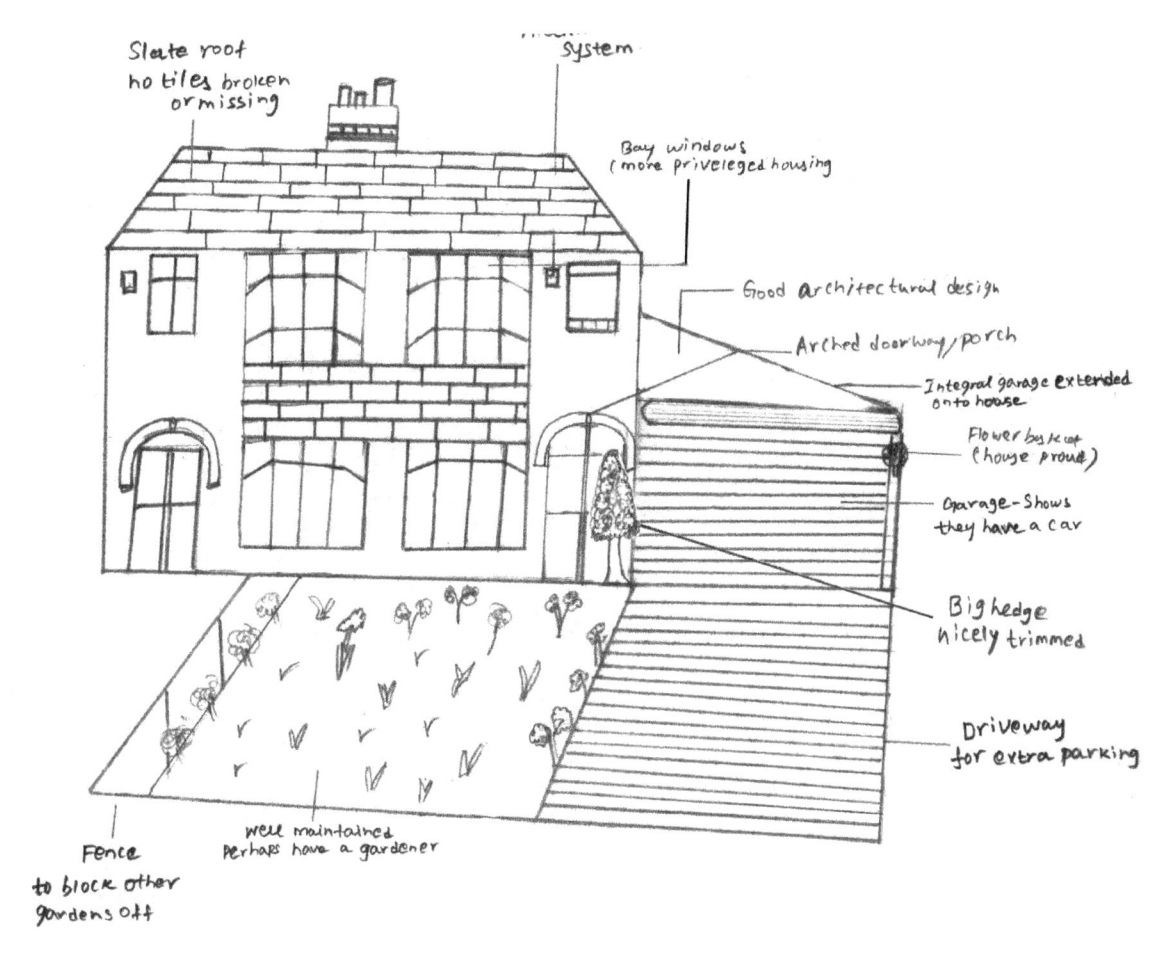

Annotated sketch of a house with the following labels:
- Slate roof no tiles broken or missing
- [...] system
- Bay windows (more privileged housing)
- Good architectural design
- Arched doorway/porch
- Integral garage extended onto house
- Flower basket (house proud)
- Garage – shows they have a car
- Big hedge nicely trimmed
- Driveway for extra parking
- Well maintained perhaps have a gardener
- Fence to block other gardens off

Section 2 This is another attractive residential area, with the larger houses mainly on the west side of the road, next to the country park. The table shows that 98% of the land next to the road has detached or semi-detached houses. Many of these were built to individual designs and are typical of inter-war ribbon developments along main roads leading out of town.

Some of Rochdale's best houses are on its rural-urban fringe.

Section 3 This section is very different to the first two. This is one of Rochdale's outer suburbs and terraced housing has replaced the detached and semi-detached dwellings. Also, their construction materials are clearly much cheaper. Section 3 is dominated by a large secondary school on the east side and an M62 flyover. There is constant traffic noise from the motorway and this may explain why there is so much derelict land. There is a mix of land use in this section, including a car showroom, a petrol station, an electricity sub-station and some old industrial buildings.

Area around the M62 motorway fly-over bridge.

Section 4 This is clearly a zone of transition. Abandoned mills have been demolished, but not all the available brownfield sites have been redeveloped. This means there are several derelict, heavily littered open spaces. There is some pebbled-dashed semi-detached housing dating from the 1940s/1950s. This is in a generally poor condition. The edge of a very large council estate (now re-classified as 'social housing') is on the west side of the main road. New low-rise blocks of flats occupy some of the land vacated by the mills.

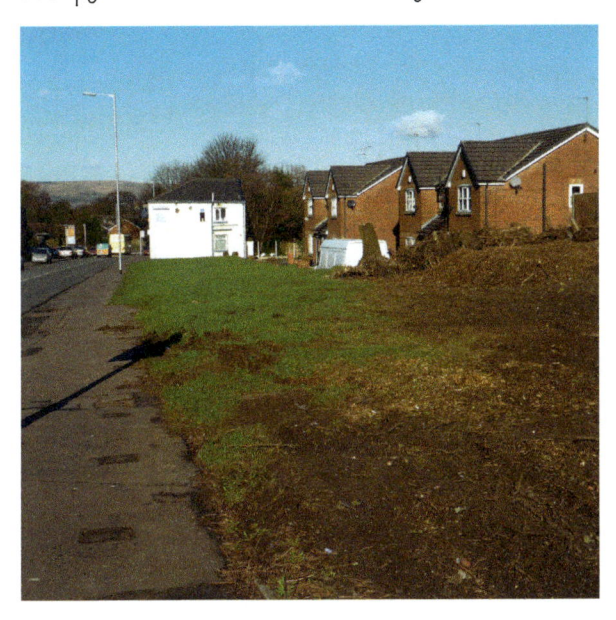

A zone of transition. It has some redevelopment, but still lots of open spaces which are unattractive and often littered.

Section 5 This is a continuation of section 4's zone of urban decay and redevelopment. There are no detached or semi-detached houses here, because all of the dwellings are terraced. Some of these are quite small, old, stone-built and attractive. But the overall 'feel' to this area is very depressing because it is so much in need of revitalisation. Its amenities include a church, a library and a small park.

This is 'terraced-house land', and looks quite run-down.

Section 6 This section contains a broad mix of housing, and many of the older terraced houses are old enough to have been built to accommodate workers in nearby mills and factories. Some of these mills can still be clearly seen behind the rows of terraces. The Kingsway/Queensway dual-carriageway ring road cuts across Oldham Road at the mid-point of this section.

Area of mixed terraced housing and industry around the Oldham Road junction with Kingsway/Queensway.

Sections 7 and 8 These are crossed by the Rochdale Canal and the railway. This obviously used to be a very active industrial part of the town, but its old mills, derelict land and closed shops now show that this section of the transect is no longer prosperous. A retail park has accelerated the decline of some of its smaller, traditional businesses. This is very much a twilight zone, in urgent need of inward investment and environmental greening.

The disused Rochdale Canal. The brownfield sites of the demolished mills have been redeveloped and now have new houses on them.

Section 9 This is the Drake Street section of the transect, which lies within the Central Business District zone. It is very near the heart of town, the Esplanade, which has a Grade 1 listed town hall and many impressive commercial buildings. Drake Street used to be the heart of Rochdale's shopping precinct, and its businesses were famous for selling high quality goods such as furniture and women's clothing. The many closed shops show that most of its trade has now moved elsewhere. This decline started in the 1960s, when large modern anchor stores were built in other areas such as Yorkshire Street. Drake Street has never recovered from this development.

Drake Street's closed and cut-price shops.

Data analysis and evaluation

This transect was only 3.5 km long, but it did highlight many striking contrasts. Its first two sections formed part of Rochdale's rural–urban fringe and their housing stock proved to be both attractive and well maintained. Section 3 was the first true urban zone, the start of its suburbs. It was one of many areas to show the scars of the town's once thriving industries, centred particularly around the canal and the railway. This evidence of urban decay continued right to the end of the transect, and the shuttered business premises on Drake Street.

Enquiry conclusions

Three questions were included in this piece of research. I will answer each question in turn.

Question 1: Does Rochdale have a Central Business District, with land uses that are less common than in its other zones?

Answer: Yes.

The transect survey showed that section 9 had the highest percentage of shops and one of the highest clusters of public buildings, services and entertainment facilities. Nearby section 8 had the second highest percentage of shops. Some other sections also included a significant number of shops, but this is probably because the transect was along a main road passing through residential areas. It is to be expected that we find shops on busy roads where there is both car and pedestrian traffic.

Question 2: Do Rochdale's industry and housing concentrate in certain parts of the town?

Answer: Yes.

Sections 1 and 2 were typical of a rural–urban fringe zone because they had larger and much higher quality housing. Then came the suburbs. The inner areas had a wider mix of housing. Much of this was terraced, and the semi-detached houses were of a generally poorer quality. Some of the inner suburb housing formed part of a large estate of social housing.

Question 3: Is Rochdale's outer zone a typical rural–urban fringe area?

Answer: Yes.

All the transect sections except the first two were clearly in decline due to the collapse of Rochdale's traditional textile and engineering industries. The town's current unemployment rate is the highest in the Greater Manchester conurbation, and the amount of local and government funding needed to reverse its effects simply isn't available in the post-recession UK.

These questions were included to make it easier to test the enquiry hypothesis: that Rochdale's town structure is typical of UK industrial settlements. The answers to all three questions suggest that this transect was a sensible choice because it provided sufficient evidence to test the hypothesis. Its early and last sections closely matched the CBD and rural-urban fringe zones shown in my diagram. Sections 1 and 2 included countryside and commuter housing along the main road and on the edge of town. At its centre (section 9), shops, services, entertainments and public buildings totally replaced housing. In the sections in between, there were mixed zones of housing, industry and transport land uses. Most of these form zones of transition, where not enough urban renewal has taken place yet.

I can now conclude that the aim of this fieldwork enquiry has been fully met.

Enquiry evaluation

Although I believe that my enquiry was successful, I think its data could have been made more accurate and comprehensive. This could have been achieved in these three ways:

1. We only recorded land use at ground level. This means that we didn't discover how the upper storeys of buildings were used. For example, there are a lot of shops along Oldham Road, and many of these will have flats above them for their owners to live in. That means the housing part of our survey must have been incomplete.
2. We only recorded land uses immediately next to the two transect roads. This means that we couldn't include the land uses behind them. The transect shows many shops along Oldham Road itself, but we can't be certain that they are the only ones in the immediate area.
3. Our transect only surveyed part of the south side of Rochdale. This means that a lot of the town was left out. One of Rochdale's most obvious landscape features is the Severn Sisters blocks of high-rise flats, but these are outside our survey area.

Physical geography GCSE model study: Coastal defences and processes

A model physical geography fieldwork enquiry examining the Holderness coast by a GCSE student

LEARNING OBJECTIVE

✓ To be able to complete a physical geography fieldwork enquiry to a high standard.

This aim and four research questions were agreed during our first visit to the Holderness coast.

Aim: To investigate coastal processes and interventions on the central Holderness coast.

QUESTIONS

1. What natural processes are active on the Hornsea/Mappleton stretch of the Holderness coast?
2. What evidence is there for these processes?
3. What measures have been taken to protect this stretch of coastline against these processes?
4. How effective have these measures been in protecting this coast?

The geographical context of my enquiry

Coastal erosion is a major issue along many parts of the UK's coastline. Holderness is one of our most vulnerable stretches of coast, which makes it an ideal location for my study. My research about this North Sea coast has revealed several pieces of useful information:

- The headland of Flamborough Head, at the northern tip of the Holderness coast, is made of hard chalk rock. This is why it has been able to resist sea erosion, juts out into the sea and has several caves, arches and stacks.
- The long middle section of the Holderness coast has much softer material, called boulder clay. This was only deposited at the end of the Ice Age. The sea has eroded this clay further inland by 4 kilometres since Roman times. In a really stormy year, the whole coast can retreat by up to 10 metres. The average annual rate of retreat is 3 metres, which makes Holderness the fastest eroding coast in the whole of Europe. Over the centuries, this erosion has led to the total loss of nearly 30 villages. Four of these are now at the bottom of the sea off Hornsea and Mappleton.
- At the southern tip of Holderness is Spurn Head. This is a narrow, curving spit on the north bank of the Humber Estuary. It is due to deposition, not erosion.
- The link between all three parts of this coast is longshore drift – the constant transportation (movement) of eroded beach material southwards due to the northeasterly prevailing winds, wave movement and offshore currents.

- Much of the time, the waves along this coastline are what are called destructive waves. They increase coastal erosion because they break heavily downwards onto the beach. Also, their retreating swash movement removes the material already loosened by the waves, then transports it out to sea.

I have also discovered that the rate of coastal erosion can be reduced by 'hard engineering' structures such as sea walls, rock armour and groynes. The recent Shoreline Management Plan for Holderness aims to safeguard Hornsea (population 8432 at the national census in 2011) for at least another 100 years. Mappleton (population now less than 100) is also being protected, but mainly because of the important north-south coastal B1242 road which passes through it. The plan says that it simply isn't possible to protect the whole of the Holderness coast – only its most important places: those where people live, work and have to travel. Hornsea's main sea defence is its strong, high promenade. At Mappleton, it cost US$ 3million to put two lines of huge granite boulders along the beach and more boulders to make rock groynes.

Hornsea's location

The regional map shows that Hornsea is at latitude 53° 55' N, longitude 0° 10' W and is on the coast of the East Riding of Yorkshire.

The Ordnance Survey 1:25 000 map extract shows both of my enquiry locations. Hornsea beach is in grid square 2147 and the Mappleton shore is at GR229439.

HORNSEA
The Leys
B1242
Cottage Hospital
School
Hall Garth Park
Moat
Liby
Pol Sta
Mkt
Hotel
Hornsea Sands
PC
Pipe Lines
IRB Sta
Groynes
FBs
Cemy
Cross
Sch
Stream
Dike
Superstore
Hornsea Burton Rd
Swan Island
Kirkholme Nab
Mere
Mill Hill
Caravan Parks
Beverley Farm
Carr Farm
F Sta
PO
Hornsea Burton
Lelley Bridge
Cherry Garths
Hornsea Bridge
Medieval Village of Southorpe (site of)
Southorpe
Southorpe Farm
Retail Park
Foss Dike
South Cliff
Mean High Water
Mean Low Water
CH
Hornsea Lakes
Southorpe Grange
Trans Pennine Trail
Hornsea Rail Trail
Hull Road
Acre Dike
Willow Garth
Rolston Cliff
Rolston Sands
Sea Field
Rolston Field
Braemar Farm
Home Farm
Rolston Seats
Hornsea Golf Club
Rolston
Grange Farm
Rolston Stud
Rolston Hall
FB
Sea Field
Mappleton Cliff
Mappleton Sands
Acredike Lands
North Field
Euber Hill
Pp Sta (dis)
Sea View Farm
Hill Farm
Eelmere Well
Sewage Works
Scardale Hill
Ardnadam
Wr Twr
Seats Hill
Seats Hill Grange
Manor Farm
Middle Farm
Middle Field
Manor Farm
Vic
Mill Farm
Mappleton
Broom Hill
Rosy Closes
Road
48
47
46
45
44
20
21
22
23

Health and safety issues

Coastlines are dangerous places, and this was proved on our first, introductory visit to Holderness. It was a very windy day and heavy waves were breaking on the shore – on average, as often as one every few seconds. Even though it wasn't a high tide, some of the waves were sending spray and pebbles right across the promenade. This was the prevailing east-northeasterly wind, which does most of the damage on this coast, causing people to run away to shelter.

We were told very clearly that, on both visits:

- We had to stay in our groups – so never be alone.
- There had to be a confident swimmer in each group while we were on a beach.
- We had to have our mobile phones with us all the time.
- We had to know where our teachers were and where our school's minibus was.
- We had to be extra careful on slippery surfaces – especially jagged rock armour and slimy groynes.
- We also had to watch out for poo, because people are allowed to walk their dogs on the beach during the winter months.

Data collection

Much of our data was collected through observation, discussing what we saw and talking to people. Lots of photographs were taken and some of them have been annotated and put into this section to describe the features we saw.

Our first two research questions required us to discover what natural processes occur along this coast, and find some evidence for them. This is what we discovered by observation.

Group of assorted pebbles.

There is much higher deposition of beach material on the north sides of all the groynes. There is a great assortment of pebble material on both beaches, not just the chalk eroded from Flamborough Head. This shows that the action of waves and currents is constantly moving material down the east coast from many different places further north, some much further than Flamborough.

The strength and frequency of the waves on our first visit was really awesome! Several wooden groynes had sections missing due to wave damage, which is not at all surprising. Most of the groynes had sections of lighter coloured wood, which was evidence of recent repair. We saw how easily the cliffs are being eroded and weathered. The softness of the boulder clay became obvious when we actually saw part of the cliff at Mappleton slumping, flowing down, just like a miniature waterfall. This was due to weathering processes, not sea erosion, but the effect is much the same.

One of our targets was to measure the height of the groynes above beach level at Hornsea. This would give us some exact data to back up our observations. There were no fewer than 12 of these, spaced out over almost 2 kilometres of beach. Because of this, we had to do some sampling. The table in the next part of my enquiry gives the averages of all the north and south side groyne heights which we recorded above the beach. If we had measured all the groynes, there wouldn't have been enough time to visit Mappleton, and a lot of useful information could have been missed.

Finally, we made sure we talked to some local people during our visit. We could have talked to quite a few day trippers in Hornsea, but their concern would be having a good day out, not talking about our coastal issues. Mappleton is a much more open, rural site than Hornsea and the people we came across there were mainly locals walking their dogs. They seemed a lot more relaxed and willing to talk to us than the busy family groups on a day trip to Hornsea.

Hornsea promenade/sea wall.

Data presentation

These photographs provide evidence for the first three research questions. They have been annotated to show just how much we were able to observe.

Part of the Hornsea beach sea wall

Strong steps down to the beach

Granite rock armour to reduce the power of the waves

South side of groyne

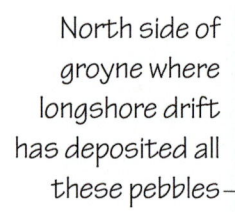

North side of groyne where longshore drift has deposited all these pebbles

All of Hornsea's groynes have strong concrete blocks to link them to the sea wall

Groyne with sections missing.

Groyne section number	Groyne height above beach on north side (cm)	Groyne height above beach on south side (cm)
(Sea wall) 1	23	90
2	70	110
3	88	94
4	95	106
5	115	125
6	125	138
7 (Sea)	131	140

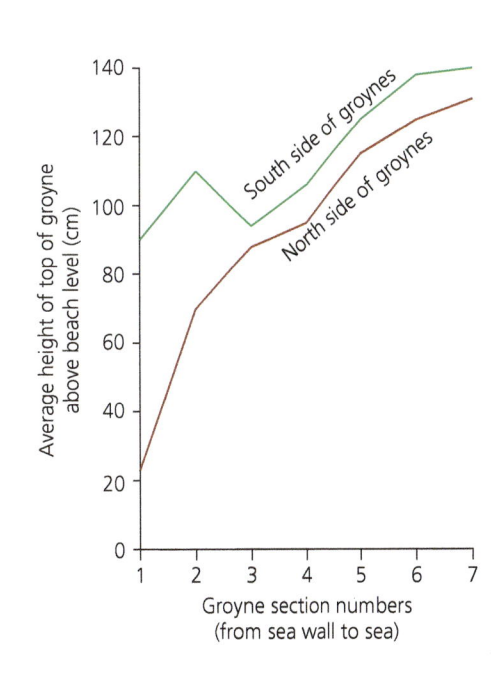

Mappleton's rock groyne.

Granite rock armour | Part of the beach | Slumped edge of boulder clay cliff

Marram grass, planted to make the shore more stable

This huge amount of boulder clay has slumped down from the cliff face

The boulder clay is soft, moist and full of small pieces of rock

Edge of fence – the rest was lost when the cliff was eroded

These boulder clay blocks will break up and be carried out to sea

These are some of the helpful comments we noted down when we talked to the people in Mappleton:

- 'I moved here eight years ago. My bungalow is right over there and before I bought it, I worked out it would be 100 years before it fell into the sea.'
- 'I'm quite near the beach. I bought the Old Post Office and turned it into this small cafe. I've no regrets – even if the sea does swallow it all up after I've gone.'
- 'Farming is the big thing here – and the car showroom in the village, of course. We'll keep on farming as long as we can because the land here is so flat and fertile.'
- 'Mappleton has lost some of its people, but the church still has services. The Archbishop of York actually joined our little congregation last Sunday.'
- 'The rock armour and the two rock groynes seem to be protecting the village OK, but look down along the coast. The cliffs are disappearing there before your very eyes!'

The few local people we managed to talk to in Hornsea were very positive about their town – and its future. Here are some of their comments:

- 'Hornsea must be safe now. Have you seen the new houses they're building all over the place?'
- 'I'm glad I bought when I did. House prices are really on the up.'
- 'I think Hornsea's safe now. They've done a wonderful job over the promenade and the place is buzzing in summer. But I do worry that they haven't protected much of the shore around us. We could end up being Yorkshire's only holiday island!'

Data analysis and evaluation

We discovered lots of evidence of longshore drift and the strength of the wind and sea currents that cause it. These are the main pieces of evidence we discovered.

The much higher deposition of beach material on the north sides of all the groynes.

The great assortment of pebble material on both beaches, not just the chalk eroded from Flamborough Head. This shows that the action of waves and currents is constantly moving material down the east coast.

The strength and frequency of the waves on our first visit was really awesome! Several wooden groynes had sections missing due to wave damage, which is not at all surprising. Most of the groynes showed signs of recent repair.

The softness of the boulder clay became very obvious when we actually saw part of the cliff at Mappleton slumping, flowing down to the beach, like a miniature clay waterfall.

The table and the compound line graph in the last section show that there is a height difference between the northern and southern groyne-side measurements. This was quite big on some groynes. It also happened on every groyne we measured. And it happened the whole length of each groyne from the sea wall down the beach to the sea. One of the piles of pebbles on the northern side was so high that it reached the top of the groyne. Any more pebbles would have toppled over onto the other side. All these pebble deposits on the same side of all the groynes could only have been caused by one process: longshore drift due to the prevailing winds and sea currents from the north-east. We could clearly see all the waves coming onto the beach from the same northerly direction.

Our talks with local people helped us to answer the last question. Although some of them still have concerns about how effective the groynes and rock armour had been, most agree that the promenade sea wall at Hornsea was doing a fantastic job in protecting the town. Their main concerns were about the beaches, which were not protected at all. The policy there seems to be to let nature take its course! They thought the rock armour was effective, but not long enough. The strong waves simply washed around the end boulders, then right up to the base of the cliff. We could see a notch eroded at the bottom of one of the cliffs where this must have happened very recently.

Enquiry conclusions

My enquiry has four research questions.

Research question 1: What natural processes are active on the Hornsea/Mappleton stretch of the Holderness coast?

Answer: The secondary sources we researched provided lots of information about the geology and the history of this stretch of coast, including its main natural processes like longshore drift.

Research question 2: What evidence is there for these processes?

Answer: We discovered lots of evidence! The main evidence was the deposits on one side of the groynes, and the wind and the waves from one direction. It all added up to longshore drift – from the northeast.

Research question 3: What measures have been taken to protect this stretch of coastline against these processes?

Answer: We recorded the long, high promenade and many wooden groynes at Hornsea, as well as the rock armour and groynes made of huge granite boulders at Mappleton. We also noted that all these defences have been part of this coast's Shoreline Management Plan.

Research question 4: How effective have these measures been in protecting this coast?

Answer: The promenade sea wall has definitely saved Hornsea from being washed away. It is immensely strong and has been made into an all-weather tourist feature. Its design has even won some national awards. The rock armour and groynes have also helped, by absorbing a lot of the power of the waves before they strike the sea wall. An obvious problem is that the sea could erode inland to the north and the south of the town, where there are almost no sea defences. Eventually, the sea could link up with Hornsea Mere lake – and completely surround the town.

The aim of this Physical Geography Enquiry was to investigate coastal processes and interventions on the central Holderness coast. My primary data and secondary research mean that I could fulfil both aims and collect proof of what I have discovered. I'm sure my enquiry wasn't perfect, but I think it worked quite well.

Enquiry evaluation

I think we should have used a questionnaire. This would have made us more organised when talking to the local people. We simply didn't realise how much they would be willing to tell us. We just chatted to them, and proper interviews would probably have been more useful for our enquiry.

We could also have measured some beach profile gradients. Our school has the basic equipment to do this (a tape measure, ranging poles and a clinometer) but our Year 11 group is quite small, which meant we couldn't do everything we would have liked to. Perhaps I'll be able to get some beach profile data for Hornsea from the Internet.

Acknowledgements of help received

Apart from my teachers, I would like to thank the people we met during our visits – especially the retired teacher who owns the cafe at Mappleton. She gave us lots of local information.

GCSE exam-style questions

LEARNING OBJECTIVES
✓ To know what types of GCSE examination questions are based on enquiry fieldwork.
✓ To understand how GCSE examination questions are marked.
✓ To be able to increase your grade potential by preparing effectively for GCSE examination questions.

Questions about health and safety issues

Question 1

Identify **two** possible risks of carrying out a fieldwork investigation in the area shown in **either** photograph A **or** photograph B. [2]

△ Photograph A

△ Photograph B

Question 2

Identify **three** possible risks of carrying out a fieldwork investigation in **either** a busy urban street **or** on the edge of a village in an area of both arable and pastoral farming. [3]

Question 3

What risk assessment was carried out for your fieldwork enquiry to reduce potential hazards during the collection of primary data? [2]

Question about aim, hypothesis and research question setting

Question 4

Underline the correct word in bold print in this statement:

'The more rounded pebbles usually cluster where there is faster-flowing water' is an example of a fieldwork enquiry **aim**/**hypothesis**/**question**. [1]

Questions about enquiry location and geographical context

Question 5

Write down the title of your fieldwork enquiry, then explain why the location or locations chosen for it were considered suitable for relevant data collection. [2]

Question 6

a) Describe one type of map used to locate your fieldwork study. [1]

b) Explain why you decided to use that type of map. [2]

Question 7

Write down the title of your fieldwork enquiry, then outline the geographical model or ideas on which your enquiry was based. [2]

Questions about data collection and reliability

Question 8

Write **any two** of these units in their most appropriate cells in this table: cm, m, m^2 and °. [2]

Type of data	Unit
Area of a quadrat used for pebble sampling	
Diameter of a pebble	
Gradient of a river bank's slope	
Height of a beach groyne	

Question 9

Data collected as part of a fieldwork enquiry can be classified as 'primary' or 'secondary'. Complete this table by putting a tick (✓) in the correct column to show whether each item is **Primary** or **Secondary** data. [4]

Data collection item	Primary	Secondary
A questionnaire that you devised, then used during your interviews		
A village's population census data that you downloaded from the Internet		
Changing water depth across a stream measured by another student in your group		
Postcards bought from a local shop, then annotated by you		

Question 10

List **three** topics or types of question that it might be unwise to include in a questionnaire. [3]

Question 11

Explain how using a geology map is likely to prove helpful in fieldwork investigations. [3]

Question 12

Explain how these pieces of equipment can be used to measure a series of gradients: a clinometer, a tape measure and ranging poles. You may include a diagram in your answer. [4]

Question 13

a) Describe how you used **one** primary data collection method for your fieldwork enquiry. [2]

b) Explain why you considered it necessary to use this method. [2]

Question 14

a) Describe **one** sampling technique that was used in **one** of your fieldwork enquiries. [2]

b) Explain why this sampling technique was adopted for use in that enquiry. [2]

c) Suggest **one** possible disadvantage of using that particular sampling technique. [1]

Question 15

A flow meter stopped working properly while students were measuring the velocity of a river. Describe how they could have obtained this information in another way. [2]

Question 16

Suggest **two** possible advantages of using electronic devices over more traditional data collection/recording methods. [2]

Question 17

Write down the title of your fieldwork enquiry, then explain how the way that you collected fieldwork data could have been improved. [4]

Questions about data presentation

Question 18

Plot this information on the bar graph below: Hacheston - population 345. [3]

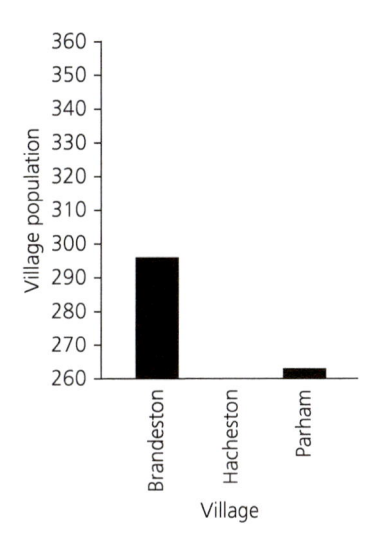

Question 19

As part of a fieldwork enquiry, a student recorded these air temperature readings at hourly intervals. Complete this line graph, using the information in the table. [2]

Time	Temperature (°C)
10 am	13
11 am	15
12 noon	17
1 pm	18
2 pm	19
3 pm	20
4 pm	19
5 pm	17

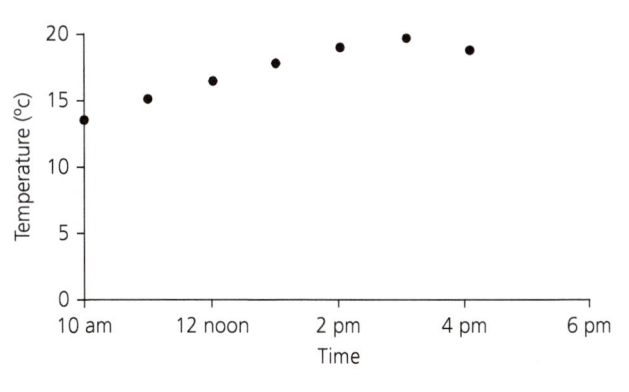

Question 20

For **any two** of these types of data, name **one** method that would be suitable for presenting it in a fieldwork enquiry.

a) Changing land use between two survey locations.

b) A series of important events that occurred in a town's history.

c) Data that shows how the volume of traffic changed during every hour between 8 am and 8 pm.

d) Data showing the *proportion* of each type of vehicle that formed part of a traffic census. [2]

Question 21

State one type of technique used in your enquiry to present data, then evaluate the usefulness of that technique for displaying the data you collected. [2]

Questions about data evaluation and reliability

Question 22

a) Draw a line of best fit on this scatter graph to show the relationship between distance from a town centre and number of pedestrians walking past a survey point. [2]

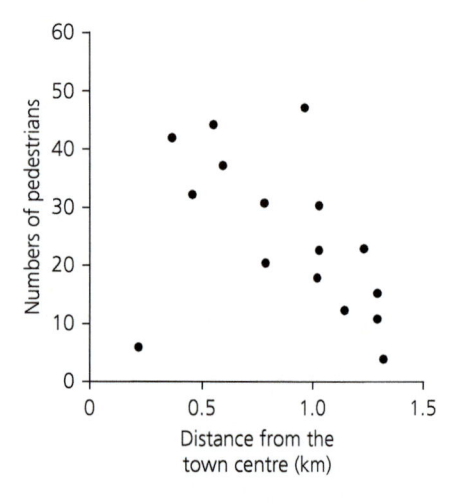

b) Describe the relationship between distance from the town centre and the number of pedestrians as shown by your completed graph. [2]

Question 23

This table shows data collected as part of a fieldwork enquiry.

Distance from sea wall (in m)	Number of pebbles in sample area
5	22
10	27
15	32
20	44
25	63
30	72
35	78
40	104
45	122
50	74
55	63

a) Calculate the **mean** of the data set shown in this table. [1]

b) Calculate the **mode** of the data set shown in this table. [1]

c) Calculate the **median** of the data set shown in this table. [1]

Question 24

Suggest **one** reason why a student might choose to use the median figure of a data set instead of its mean. [2]

Question 25

The information in this table was collected to investigate the total number of shops in towns within an enquiry area.

Name of settlement	Number of shops in that settlement
Ampleburgh	18
Cold Harbour	78
Denton	6
Grimley	45
Limworth	23
North Heapey	33
Preston	29
Riversway	17
Tinbridge	44
West Walling	31

a) Calculate the upper quartile of this data set, showing clearly how you arrived at your answer. [3]

b) Calculate the interquartile range of the shop survey data, also showing clearly how you arrived at your answer. [3]

Questions about enquiry conclusions and evaluation

Question 26

Write down the title of your fieldwork enquiry, then outline the main results and conclusions of your enquiry. [4]

Question 27

Write down the title of your fieldwork investigation, then evaluate the relative importance of the qualitative and quantative data used in reaching your enquiry conclusions. [8]

Answers available at www.collins.co.uk/FWGCSEGeo

Glossary

aim a way of stating an enquiry's purpose

annotation detailed information added to an illustration

bar graph a graph with columns that show data that does not change over time

best-fit line a line added to a scatter graph which passes as close to as many of the plotted points as possible

brownfield site land that becomes available for re-use after the demotion of builings

calipers instrument to measure pebble size

Central Business District the zone in which most of a town's business, recreation and transport facilities are located

choropleth map a map with colour shading between its plotted lines to show a distribution pattern

clinometer an instrument for measuring gradient angles

commuter a person who travels daily to work

contour a line on a map that links places that have the same height above sea level

correlation coefficient a mathematical calculation that indicates the strength of the link between two sets of data

cross-section a diagram showing how the height of the land changes along a transect

derelict describes property that has been abandoned and allowed to deteriorate

description providing information about a place or event, but not suggesting any reasons for why or how it has occurred

desire-line map a map that uses straight lines to show the movement of people or goods between places

destructive waves waves that can erode a coast – because they exert a powerful downward force as they break, and their strong backwash movement transports the loosened beach material out to sea

divided bar graph a circular diagram with sectors that shows the different sizes of parts within a data set

erosion the wearing away and loosening of material due to the action of moving wind, water and ice – as well as walkers' footwear

explanation stating possible reasons for a geographical fact or topic that has been described

flow line map a map that uses straight lines whose thickness is proportional to the volume of traffic along routes between places

geology the study of rocks and their impact on the landscape

GIS a computer system that can store, combine and analyse layers of different types of spatial information

grid references a system for locating places and features on a map using numbered horizontal and vertical grid lines

groyne a wall built across part of a beach to reduce longshore drift along a coast

health and safety issues potential hazards that may occur during the collection of data for an enquiry

histogram a graph that uses columns to show information that is continuous in some way

hypothesis a statement that an enquiry is designed to prove or disprove

inter-quartile range a measure of the spread of data numbers around their median figure

interview asking people to provide information needed for an enquiry

isoline map a map that has lines which join places having the same value

label brief information added to an illustration

latitude and longitude the system of locating the exact positions of places on the Earth's surface

line graph a graph that uses a line to show how data has changed over time

longshore drift the natural movement of sand and other material along a coast due to wave action and wind

mean the average number within a data set

meander a bend in a stream or river

median the central number in a data set

mode the number that occurs most often in a data set

nearest neighbour analysis a mathematical way of showing how closely located similar land uses are to each other

overlay a piece of tracing paper that shows information about an illustration without disfiguring it

pictogram a graph that uses repeated shapes or symbols instead of bars to show quantity

pie graph a circular diagram with sectors that show the different sizes of parts within a data set

population pyramid a form of bar graph that shows a population's age and gender characteristics

prevailing winds winds that blow from one particular direction for most of the time

promenade a strong, high walkway built behind a beach to stop the sea flooding the land behind it

proportional symbol a symbol whose size is directly linked to that of the data it is displaying

questionnaire a set of questions put to people as part of their interview

ranging poles two poles which are used together with a tape measure and a clinometer to obtain the gradients of slopes on beaches or valley sides

redevelopment the upgrading of urban areas to give them a new lease of life

ribbon development urbanisation that takes place along roads leading out of a town

river cliff the steep bank on the outside of a meander

rock armour large boulders placed on a shore to reduce the power of oncoming waves and the rate of erosion along it

rural-urban fringe the zone at the outer edge of a built-up area; the place where town and country meet

scale the relationship between the actual size of an area on the ground and a map's representation of the same area

scatter graph a diagram used to show the strength of the link (relationship) between two sets of data

settlement the term for a built-up area of any size

site the place where a settlement was first established

slip-off slope the gently-sloping inner bank of a meander

slumping loose material falling off a cliff face

spot height a point on a map that shows its exact height above sea level

suburbs the residential zones that are built as a town expands outwards

symbol a colour, shape, line or letter used to locate a type of feature on a map

timeline a way of displaying the timing and sequence of important events in the history of a place

transect a section that shows how human or physical features change across an area

transportation the movement of material, such as pebbles, by flowing water

triangular graph a type of diagram that allows three sets of data to be plotted against each other

urban describes built-up areas

urbanisation the expansion of an urban area

zone a part of an urban area that has particular functions such as housing and industry

Index

A
aims of an enquiry 58
annotating 18–19, 57

B
bar graphs 7
basic skills practice exercises 23–36
best-fit lines 47
Brighouse, West Yorkshire 37–43
brownfield sites 58, 79–80

C
callipers 70
calculating percentages 24
Central Business District 37, 65, 71
choropleth maps 16–17
clinometer 21–22
commuting 68, 72, 77
conclusions 64
contours 16, 21
compass directions 12
correlation coefficients 47
cross-sections 20–21
Croyde, north Devon 49–51

D
data collation 6
data collection 40, 60
data evaluation 63
data presentation 63
data reliability 61
desire-line maps 48
destructive waves 84
distributions on maps 52
divided bar graphs 8
drawing sketches 19–20
drawing sketches from photographs 54

E
enquiry context 59
enquiry evaluation 64
enquiry hypotheses and questions 59, 64
enquiry location 59–60
enquiry sequence 57
erosion 66, 83–84

F
flow line maps 48

G
GCSE-style examination questions 94–100
geological maps 51
GIS maps 48–49
Goole, East Riding of Yorkshire 25–26
grid references 15–16
groynes 61, 86–93

H
health and safety issues 62
histograms 8–9
Holderness, East Riding of Yorkshire 83–84, 92–93
Hornsea, East Riding of Yorkshire 83–84, 87–88, 91–92
hypotheses of an enquiry 59

I
interviewing 45–46
isoline maps 16

L
labelling 18
latitude and longitude 44
line graphs 10
longshore drift 83, 92

M
Mappleton, East Riding of Yorkshire 83–84, 87, 90–93
map symbols 11, 27–28, 32–33
mean, median and mode 22
meanders 59, 69–70
model fieldwork enquiries 37–43

N
nearest neighbour analysis 66

O
Ordnance Survey maps, 1:25 000 scale 12, 15, 31, 60, 85
Ordnance Survey maps, 1:50 000 scale 12, 15, 26, 50, 53, 60, 73
Ordnance Survey 1:25 000 scale map symbols 32–33
Ordnance Survey 1:50 000 scale map symbols 27–28
overlays 18, 36, 57

P
photographs 18–19, 57, 60, 63
pictograms 9
pie charts 10–11
population pyramids 46
postcards 18, 57, 58, 61
prevailing winds 83, 86, 92
proportional symbols 55

Q
questionnaires 45–46
questions of an enquiry 59

R
ranging poles 21–22
redevelopment 79–80
research sample size 40
ribbon development 77
Rochdale, Greater Manchester 71–82
rock armour 84, 86, 88, 90–93
rural-urban fringe 71, 78, 81–82

S
scale and distance 12
scatter graphs 46–47
site 65
sketch maps 54
slumping 87, 92
spot heights 21
suburbs 71, 78, 81, 82
suggested fieldwork enquiries 65–70
symbols 9, 11, 27–28, 32–33

T
tables 6–7
timelines 44
transects 17, 20
transportation 83
triangular graphs 55

U
using atlas maps 16–17, 44
using GIS maps 48, 60
using Ordnance Survey maps 15–16

W
Woolacombe, north Devon 49–50

Z
zones 37, 71

Acknowledgements

The publishers wish to thank the following for permission to reproduce imagery. Every effort has been made to trace copyright holders and to obtain their permission for the use of copyright materials. The publishers will gladly receive any information enabling them to rectify any error or omission at the first opportunity:

(t=top, b=bottom, r=right, l=left)
This product uses map data licensed from Ordnance Survey © Crown copyright and database rights (2015) Ordnance Survey (100018598)
Images not listed here were created by the team at Collins and are therefore © Collins Bartholomew Ltd 2016

Cover & p1: Chris Frost/Shutterstock, and © Crown copyright and database rights (2015) Ordnance Survey (100018598)

15: base files Abert/Shutterstock and Kubko/Shutterstock
16: base files Abert/Shutterstock and Kubko/Shutterstock
18 and 19t: travelib Europe/Alamy Stock Photo
19b: Ewelina Wachala/Shutterstock
20: base files Abert/Shutterstock and Kubko/Shutterstock
21: base files Abert/Shutterstock and Kubko/Shutterstock
22r: Royal Geographical Society (with IBG)

26: © Crown copyright and database rights (2015) Ordnance Survey (100018598)
27 and 28: © Crown copyright and database rights (2015) Ordnance Survey (100018598)
29: A.P.S. (UK)/Alamy Stock Photo
31: © Crown copyright and database rights (2015) Ordnance Survey (100018598)
32 and 33: © Crown copyright and database rights (2015) Ordnance Survey (100018598)
34: Nick Carraway/Alamy Stock Photo
36t: David Robinson / Alamy Stock Photo
36b: Peter Noyce PLB/Alamy Stock Photo

41: Jack and Meg Gillett
42: Jack and Meg Gillett
43: Jack and Meg Gillett

49: ian woolcock/Shutterstock
50: © Crown copyright and database rights (2015) Ordnance Survey (100018598)
51: Permit Number CP16/036 British Geological Survey © NERC 2016. All rights reserved. © Crown copyright and database rights (2015) Ordnance Survey (100018598)
52: Pedro Luz Cunha/Alamy Stock Photo
53: © Crown copyright and database rights (2015) Ordnance Survey (100018598)
54t: Paul Tavener/Alamy Stock Photo
54b: base files Abert/Shutterstock and Kubko/Shutterstock

57: base files Abert/Shutterstock and Kubko/Shutterstock
61: base file Kubko/Shutterstock

73: © Crown copyright and database rights (2015) Ordnance Survey (100018598)
78t: Jack and Meg Gillett
78b: Jack and Meg Gillett
79t: Jack and Meg Gillett
79b: Jack and Meg Gillett
80t: Jack and Meg Gillett
80b: Jack and Meg Gillett
81: Jack and Meg Gillett

85: © Crown copyright and database rights (2015) Ordnance Survey (100018598)
86: Jack and Meg Gillett
87: Jack and Meg Gillett
88t: Jack and Meg Gillett
88b: Jack and Meg Gillett
89: Jack and Meg Gillett
90t: Jack and Meg Gillett
90b: Jack and Meg Gillett
91: Jack and Meg Gillett

94t: BANANA PANCAKE/Alamy Stock Photo
94b: Kevin Eaves/Shutterstock

[Note: the sample student responses in the text have been written by the authors]